A Day at the Races

To my good friends &
neighbours – John
& Marge Boone
with warm wishes
Jack Fitzgerald
July 2016

Other Jack Fitzgerald books from Creative Book Publishing

Amazing Newfoundland Stories	ISBN 0-920021-36-0	$9.95
Strange But True Newfoundland Stories	ISBN 0-920021-57-3	$9.95
Newfoundland Fireside Stories	ISBN 0-920021-78-6	$9.95
Where Angels Fear To Tread	ISBN 1-895387-49-3	$11.95
Another Time, Another Place	ISBN 1-895387-75-2	$11.95
The Hangman is Never Late	ISBN 1-894294-02-5	$12.95
Beyond Belief	ISBN 1-894294-31-9	$12.95
Jack Fitzgerald's Notebook	ISBN 1-894294-40-8	$12.95
Beyond the Grave	ISBN 1-894294-54-8	$12.95

Ask your favourite bookstore or order directly from the publisher.

Creative Book Publishing
P.O. Box 8660
36 Austin Street
St. John's, NL
A1B 3T7

phone: (709) 722-8500
fax: (709) 579-7745
e-mail: books@printatlantic.com
URL: www.nfbooks.com

Please add $5.00 Canadian for shipping and handling and taxes on single book orders and $1.00 for each additional book.

A DAY AT THE RACES

The St. John's Regatta Story

Jack Fitzgerald

St. John's, Newfoundland and Labrador
2003

Le Conseil des Arts | The Canada Council
du Canada | for the Arts

We acknowledge the support of The Canada Council for the Arts for our publishing program.

We acknowledge the financial support of the Government of Canada through the Book Publishing Industry Development Program (BPIDP) for our publishing program.

Cover Design: Maurice Fitzgerald
∞ Printed on acid-free paper

Published by
CREATIVE PUBLISHERS
an imprint of CREATIVE BOOK PUBLISHING
a division of Creative Printers and Publishers Limited
an Print Atlantic associated company
P.O. Box 8660, St. John's, Newfoundland A1B 3T7

First Edition
Typeset in 11 point New Baskerville

Printed in Canada by:
PRINT ATLANTIC

National Library of Canada Cataloguing in Publication

Fitzgerald, Jack, 1945-
        A day at the races / Jack Fitzgerald.

ISBN 1-894294-64-5

        1. Royal St. John's Regatta--History. 2. Boats and boating--Newfoundland and Labrador--St. John's--History. 3. St. John's (N.L.)--Social life and customs. I. Title.

GV776.15.N48F57 2003   797.1'4'097181   C2003-903368-6

DEDICATION

This book is dedicated to Bridie Cole who made such a magnificent contribution to the youth of St. John's during the 1940s and 1950s. It's hard to imagine a youth growing up in St. John's in those years who did not at one time or another encounter Bridie Cole. She taught children at Bannerman and Victoria Parks to swim, taught the boys to kick a soccer ball, hit a baseball and initiated many activities for girls. In addition, Bridie took many kids to the Regatta for their first time. Bridie Cole organized annually the popular Playground's Radio Show. Among those who benefited from Bridie's encouragement and help was Newfoundland's Mary Lou Collins — a first class singer who appeared on the top television shows in Canada and the United States including the Jack Benny Show and the Bob Hope Show. Bridie was known for her kindness and many people turned to her in times of need as they would to a politician or clergyman.

Bridie, we loved ya then and we loves ya now!

TABLE OF CONTENTS

INTRODUCTION xi

CHAPTER ONE

AMAZING REGATTA HISTORY 1
Regatta Feelings at Beaumont Hamel; Germans Battle
British at Regatta; The Lightest Boat; The Strangest Boat;
The Death Boat; Forgotten Hero; 9:13 Twist; Sexton's
Brush With Death; The Regatta of the Six Brides; The
Blue Peter; Novelty Attractions; The Greasy Pig and
More!; Oriental Palace; The Platform; The Tobacco
Regattas; Winners Out!; The Steward's the Boss; The
1820's Road; Brewin's Gun; The Bard of Prescott at the
Races; The Bounce Boat Races; The Victoria Carriage;
Generous Builder; Silver Cups; US Military Aids
Regatta; An American First; Religion at the Regatta; First
Broadcast of the Regatta.

CHAPTER TWO

REGATTA HUMOUR 35
Regatta Justice; The Gull and Mrs. Reid; Three Stooges
Day at the Races; Regatta Motto; The Gambler; Captain
Horse and Jinx Marines; Toads, Rattlesnakes and
Politicians; Keep Off The Grass; Our President; Torbay
Show; Hard Times; Pondside Wit; War Games; Old
Benedicts; Wet Paint; Poor Rower; An Honourable
Soaking; The Cow; Lost on the Pond; Dum Da Diddley.

CHAPTER THREE

SOOKS OF THE REGATTA 51

No Phil Brown — No Race; Torbay's Turn; Blackhead; The *Native*; Angry Outer Cove; Targeted Committee Member; The Clapp Trap; Fixed Race; Sabotage; Brawl; Regatta Nearly Collapsed; Politics; Fans Caused Trouble; Land Dispute; Holy Cross; The Cursing Crew; The Disqualified Crew.

CHAPTER FOUR

REGATTA MYSTERIES 69

The 8:40 Record Claim!; Was the Time of 8:40 Rowed at the Races?; The Ladies Break Through; Powder Puff Brigade; Changing Boat Styles; The Unbroken 9:13; Old Course Record; Unknown Race Revealed; Near Disaster of 1944; The Earthquake, The Shower of Quartz; The First Regattas; How Many Regattas Held?; The Wednesday Tradition; The Bowring Connection; Last Will and Testament; The Name Kitty Vitty.

CHAPTER FIVE

THE MERRY REGATTA 107

Like Christmas; Fans on the Lake; The Farms; Music and Dancing; Visitors; From Washington; Dynamite Dunn; The Boston Visitor; Lost an Oar; The Americans.

CHAPTER SIX

BOATS AND BUILDERS 121

First Boats; Nineteenth Century Boats and Builders; Phil Mahoney; Boat Sizes; It's the Boats, Not the Rowers; The Longboats; Sexton; Rendell; Rendell and Sexton Team

Up; Genius Builder; End of the Sexton Era; Four- and
Six-Oared Races.

CHAPTER SEVEN

THE ROYAL INFLUENCE...137
Royalty and the Regatta; The Prince of Wales; A Gift for
the Prince of Wales; Another Prince Visits; Royal
Regattas; Royal Gifts; Queen Elizabeth II Visits; Andy
Wells Not Impressed!

CHAPTER EIGHT

LIQUOR HISTORY OF THE REGATTA......................................145
Liquor Consumption; Ladies Boycott; Dampened
Spirits; More Problems; Governor Loved It!; Congdon's
Spruce Beer!; Fogarty; Pooh Bah's; Shebeen Tents;
Committee Scandal; Battling Drunks; Harry Murphy's
Verse.

CHAPTER NINE

INSPIRATIONS 157
The Regatta Inspires; Dick Squires; John Coaker; The
Placentia Challenge; Dead Heats; Records; Blackhead;
Revived Regatta; The 1877 and 1977 Placentia Crews;
Shotty Rogers; The Ballad of the 9:13; Higher Levels;
Hall of Fame; Regatta Greats; Reprint of 1901 Telegram
Page on the Regatta.

INTRODUCTION

The Royal St. John's Regatta is more than a social or sporting event. Through nearly 200 years of history, the Regatta has become a Newfoundland tradition and institution. No other event can attract 50,000 people and only Christmas can compare with it as a season. It begins in mid-April when the boats first go on the pond for practice and ends on Regatta Day; weather permitting, it is usually the first Wednesday in August. Like Christmas, people and whole families plan holidays to coincide with the event. The longevity and success of the Regatta is rooted in the fact that it is a family tradition passed down from generation to generation. It is also a place where tradition and culture thrive. People love recalling its long past and are fascinated by the traditions and stories that have amassed over almost 200 years of history.

In this book I have attempted to preserve this history. In my two earlier books, *Up the Pond* and *The Stroke of Champions*, I gathered the year-by-year newspaper records for the first Regattas from 1826, the year it was first reported in the press, up to 1981. These books are now out of print. This third collection presents a very different approach. It preserves Regatta history and traditions in nine chapters with many pictures of Regattas gone by.

Chapter One deals with the amazing side of the Regatta and tells many wonderful stories ranging from the Regatta of the Six Brides to the day the German and British militaries battled on the pond. The amazing novelty booths and attractions and many of the ancient traditions are included.

Chapters Two, Three, Five, Seven, and Eight deal with the human side of the Regatta. These chapters preserve the fascinating, humourous, and intriguing anecdotes of Regatta history. Humour is dealt with in Chapter Two; stories of poor sportsmanship in Chapter Three; and the merry Regattas and interesting visitors in Chapters Five and Seven. Chapter Eight presents a history of liquor at the Regatta. The traditional arguments that stem around the length of the pond, when the Regatta started, how many actual Regattas were held are answered in Chapter Four. This chapter also questions several claims by the Regatta Committee over the past century and offers researched answers. Chapters Six and Nine deal with the boats, the builders, rowers, crews, and events that have shaped the Regatta and inspires new generations.

Still there is much of Regatta history left to tell. More in depth stories of the great rowers, crews, builders, and women participation in the Regatta are yet to be chronicled. I leave these topics for another book.

CHAPTER ONE

Amazing Regatta History

When the tents are in full swing
and the music sweetly ring
and the boiling crubeens upon the dishes
slopin'
Where the figgy duffs are seen,
that would sink a brigantine
or would gap a Yankee hatchery-ing to open!

From Johnny Burke's
Regatta Program, 1898

REGATTA FEELINGS AT BEAUMONT HAMEL

There was a heightened sense of a pending war at the Regatta of 1914. Throughout the day on Wednesday, August 5, Committee member Harold Jeans kept the crowds informed on events in Europe which led to Britain's declaration of war on Germany. Patriotism at lakeside was so high that when the Governor arrived at the Regatta, the crowds spontaneously burst into the singing of the *Ode To Newfoundland* followed by *Rule Britannia*.

Among those present that day was Regatta legend Sam Ebsary. Ebsary, since inducted into the Royal St. John's Regatta Hall of Fame, was one of the first 200 volunteers; better known as the Blue Puttees. One of the Regatta's all-time great coxswains, Sam Ebsary quickly moved up in rank from Sergeant to Second Lieutenant with the Royal Newfoundland Regiment. He was among the few that survived the Battle of Beaumont Hamel on July 1, 1916. Sombre, heartsick days followed the disaster. Ebsary often thought of home and imagined that if war had not broken out, crowds would at that time be at Quidi Vidi watching crews practice for the Regatta.

During this period an incident took place that reflected the depth of love Newfoundlander's hold for the traditional Regatta at Quidi Vidi. Darkness had fallen over the land and soldiers were sitting around at the camp-type headquarters quietly reflecting upon recent tragedies. The book, *The Fighting Newfoundlander,* described what happened that night. Colonel Nicholson wrote,

> It was nearly midnight when 2nd Lieutenant Sam Ebsary dropped out of the darkness near the entrance to re-appear with a large accordion which he had brought with him from 'A' Company's billets in the ramparts.
>
> Let one of 'D' Company's officers who was present describe the scene: "Sitting in the corner on an

empty ammunition box, he commenced to play and as the music emerged from the instrument, the sand-bagged walls of our 'HQ' seemed to fade; *The Banks of Newfoundland* rang in our ears and we saw once more the tented slopes of Quidi Vidi on Regatta Day; the *Blue Peter* had turned the buoy and the other boats were swinging into position." Less than three months later on October 12, 1916, Sam Ebsary died from wounds received in the Battle of Guencourt.

His career at the Regatta ran from 1899 to 1913. During this period he participated in every Regatta with a total of seventy-one races which included thirty-four wins, twenty-two second place spots, and eight third place fin-ishes. He was respected as the Regatta's top coxswain of that era. Few know that about twenty-five years later, a Newfoundland doctor speaking to a gathering at Cape Breton compared how Newfoundlanders feel about the St. John's Regatta by stating, "It's our Grecian Olympics, our American Fourth of July all combined into one day."

GERMANS BATTLE BRITISH AT REGATTA

Just thirteen years before the battlefront death of Ebsary, German soldiers were welcomed at the St. John's Regatta and participated in a competition against rowers from the British Navy and a crew of young cadets from St. John's.

The people of St. John's were accustomed to seeing British Navy crews compete at the historic Quidi Vidi Regatta, but a rowing crew from the German Navy was another matter. When it was announced in 1903 that the German Navy would be entering a crew in the Naval-Brigade Race at the Regatta, enthusiasm soared. People speculated on how the Germans would do against local rowers or the crew that year from the British Navy.

The German entry came as a surprise to the people of St. John's. The German Naval Gunboat, *Panther,* arrived in St. John's Harbour to take on supplies days before the Regatta. When they learned of the historic Regatta being held near the City and that the British Navy were participating, they eagerly accepted an invitation to participate.

Three crews competed in the Naval-Brigade Race: the British, the Germans, and a crew with the top rowers taken from the Church Lads Brigade and the Catholic Cadet Corps. The Germans were assigned the *Blue Peter,* the fastest boat on the pond, and gambling on the race was widespread. Even the German and British Naval Officers waged bets on the outcome. However, it soon became evident after the starting gun fired that the British were the crew to beat. They crossed over the finish line with the CLB-CCC crew in second place and the Germans a distant last. Nevertheless, the Germans were good sports and stayed at lakeside to enjoy the festivities. The German *Panthers* Brass Band enthusiastically took over music duties from Professor Power's Band in the afternoon to allow the local band members time to participate in the festive activities at lakeside.

British sailors often competed at the St. John's Regatta. In 1906 a crew of sailors from the British Warship HMS *Brilliant* rowed against the Calypso crew, and two crews of firemen from St. John's; one from Southside, the other the Central Fire Station. It was a thrilling race and attracted heavy betting. The Southside Firemen, rowing in the *Red Lion,* sparked loud cheering from the crowds as they took first place in the event.

THE LIGHTEST BOAT

The early Regattas were quaint, charming, picturesque, and extremely competitive. Their popularity was enhanced by the intriguing novel and sometimes amazing experiences and attractions that accompanied it. The combination of a sporting competition with a variety of unique side attractions made the Regatta the sporting and social event of the year and in time a truly Newfoundland Institution.

One amazing event in Regatta history was the racing of the lightest boat ever to compete on Quidi Vidi Lake. The *Columbia,* a mere thirty pounds, competed in the Regatta of 1880. This unique racer was imported from Cortez by Arthur Rendell, a prominent Regatta enthusiast of the era. It arrived in St. John's Harbour on board a cargo ship on July 27, 1880, just days before the races.

This peculiar craft was made of papier-mâshé and was christened the *Columbia* by Rendell. He then entered the craft in the single scull All-Comer's Race which was the fifth race on the Regatta Day Program. The usual heavy betting at lakeside took place and the *Columbia* was considered little more than an amusing novelty. Some who bet against the *Columbia* jokingly suggested the wind would carry her straight down the pond and out to Quidi Vidi Harbour. Others commented that high winds might keep her from even touching the water at Quidi Vidi Lake.

When Regatta Day arrived, it was one of the finest days of the season. Skies were clear and the lake was calm. Few at lakeside were smiling when the *Columbia* took an early lead and, to the surprise of many, maintained the lead throughout the entire race. The little thirty-pound wonder-boat crossed the finish line in first place defeating four others: *Ethel*, *Lottie* and two unnamed boats owned by William Hughes and Harry Tucker. The performance of such a light boat that day became an instant Regatta legend that lasted for several decades. As time progressed, however, its achievements disappeared from public memory.

THE STRANGEST BOAT

While the *Columbia* earned the record as the lightest boat ever to compete in our Regatta, the title of the most unusual race craft belongs to the *Argus*. The *Argus* competed in the Regatta of 1877. The craft was a curiosity and wonder of the day, but like the *Columbia* its memory was lost until I discovered the story in my research. The Regatta of 1877 is remembered as the year a Placentia crew brought a boat to St. John's and won the Fishermen's Race. It is also the year that a sixteen-oared boat, manned by a crew mostly from Ethiopia, competed in the St. John's Regatta.

This spectacle occurred in the Naval Race; the seventh competition of the day. Six crews participated. The boats in the race consisted of whaleboats, cutters, a gig, and the curiosity boat, *Argus*. The barge, as it was described in the *Morning Chronicle*, was one of two entrants from the paddle ship *Argus* visiting the port of St. John's that week. It bore the name *Argus* at the Regatta.

Describing the construction of the craft, the *Chronicle* stated, "The wood of which she is constructed is African, and, as it should be, is ash-and-teak, or ashantique that is the same thing. The barge belongs to the paddle-steamer *Argus*, and is, we believe, intended for landing troops in rough weather on dangerous coasts."

The newspaper noted, "She was well manned, and had a sprinkling of blameless Ethiopians among her crew, but contrived to come in as nearly last as she would well get." The *Argus* was built at Ashantee in Africa. The Naval Race was won by a whaleboat from the HMS *Belloraphen*. The *Argus* came in last.

THE DEATH BOAT

The race boat *Terra Nova* survived superstition, unpopularity, and being shunned to become one of the most successful boats of nineteenth century Regattas. Its first Regatta was the 1884 Regatta and patrons of the Races had high expectations for the new boat on the pond.

That enthusiasm was replaced with sadness and superstition, and fans leaving the Regatta that evening hoped that the boat would never again be seen in a Regatta. In the young Fishermen's Race, which got underway at 2:30 p.m., the *Terra Nova* was being rowed by the young fishermen's crew from Torbay. She was making good time when a high westward wind swept in over the pond. When the *Terra Nova* turned the buoys, she began taking on water. After passing the buoys, the cox, Pat Ryan, instructed the crew to head for shore. Just past Coaker's River, and only forty feet from shore, the *Terra Nova* went under and turned upside down. Three rowers lost their lives in what turned out to be the worst tragedy of Regatta history. (The three victims were Mogue Power, Sam Gosse, and John Martin.)

However, its builder, Phil Mahoney of Southside Road, did not lose faith in his creation. Mahoney, one of the top boat builders of nineteenth century Regattas, was convinced that bad weather and not his boat was the cause of the tragic accident. He was very proud of his new boat and reflected colonial patriotism by painting it pink, white, and green (colours of the old Newfoundland flag) and calling it the *Terra Nova*.

Some felt that he made a poor choice of a name. The original *Terra Nova* which had participated in Regattas from 1872 to 1882 had a dismal record. Indeed, in her ten year history, she registered very few wins. Mahoney was convinced his new *Terra Nova* would not be hindered by bad luck or superstition, and expected success on the pond.

After the tragedy of 1884, Mahoney studied his design during the fall and winter months while he repaired and made several adjustments to the boat. By the 1885 Regatta, the boat that townsfolk had been calling 'The Bad Luck Boat,' 'The Jinxed Boat,' and 'The Death Boat' was ready to go back on the pond. But one question remained. Would the rowers use it? Mahoney, builder of the *Volunteer* which had recorded some of the best times of the previous ten years, felt the *Terra Nova* was a much faster boat.

To give the boat a fresh new start, Mahoney renamed it *Myrtle*. While Torbay rowers shunned it for several Regattas, others took their chances with it. They were not sorry. By the end of Regatta Day 1885, Mahoney's boat was no longer 'The Jinxed Boat.' The *Myrtle* was the most successful boat of the 1885 Regatta recording an amazing eight wins and one second place honour. Even more impressive, the Outer Cove crew rowing in the *Myrtle* set a new course record of 9:20. The following year the *Myrtle*'s reputation as a winner was enhanced when she recorded twelve first place honours and the fastest time of the day; 9:35 recorded in the Fishermen's Race.

The superstition that lingered after 1884 had totally disappeared and in 1888 the Torbay crew was proud to row the fastest boat of the St. John's Regatta. However, mid-way through the race, the crew was suddenly reminded of the tragedy of 1884. Just as the Torbay crew of 1884 got in trouble while turning the buoys, the 1888 crew experienced a similar problem. The winds had increased and the *Myrtle* was taking on water as she neared Coaker's River. The crew of 1888 was faced with the same decision the rowers in the tragedy of 1884 had to consider. They chose to row harder and continue the race. Fortunately, by 1888, two rescue boats were on the pond and if any crew got in trouble, help was not far away. The crew made the finish line with the water only inches from the gunwales.

The *Gypsy*, another boat in the race, faced a more serious problem. After taking on water, one of her planks broke and the race boat had to be towed to shore by one of the rescue boats. In the Tradesmen's Race, the *Myrtle* recorded a 10:08 which was the best time of the day. Mahoney's pride of the Regatta continued its success in 1889 by recording the fastest time of the day in the four-oared contests and in 1890 racked up six wins and the fastest time of the day in the four-oared category. In 1891, the *Myrtle* had a 9:42, the fastest six-oared time of the day, as well as 10:00, the fastest time of the day in the four-oared races. This time also stands in Regatta history as the record time in the four-oared category.

In 1897, Bob Sexton remodeled the *Myrtle* and she was, "...played down to the pond by the Total Abstinence Band." A combined crew from Torbay and Outer Cove won the four-oared race in the *Myrtle*. However, the *Myrtle*'s reign as a top boat of Regatta history was at its end. Sexton had put his newly designed boat the *Glance*, a much longer and faster boat, on the pond in 1897 and she won eight of thirteen races. Over the next decade, the *Myrtle* was used as a practice boat on Quidi Vidi and St. John's Harbour.

FORGOTTEN HERO

An inmate of Her Majesty's Penitentiary in St. John's earned a pardon and early release from prison after a display of heroism at the 1884 Quidi Vidi Regatta. James Briskett was serving a jail term for assaulting a police officer but he was allowed outside on Regatta Day to perform work on the prison grounds.

A crew rowing up the pond ran into trouble near the boathouse (not current day boathouse) and sank. Briskett saw the boat going down and without hesitation went into the water in an attempt to rescue the crew. Retelling the story in a July 22, 1905, column, the *Evening Telegram* described Briskett as, "a swimmer to the manor born, a man of great strength; he cleaves the water with great strokes but the rowers had pulled their last race."

Although Briskett's efforts were unsuccessful, his display of heroism earned him the admiration of the people of St. John's. A petition to release him, signed by thousands, was presented to the Governor. A pardon was granted and crowds were on hand to applaud as the convict hero stepped out through the prison gates.

Briskett left Newfoundland for Boston and fought with the Northern Troops in the American Civil War. Following the war, he engaged in business activities and returned to St. John's to attend later Regattas as a wealthy man.

9:13 TWIST

In the Fishermen's Race of 1901, the Torbay crew won with Outer Cove coming in a close second. The crew that won the Tradesmen's race that day was eligible to row in the championship contest by virtue of their time recorded in the *Blue Peter*.

Competitiveness was very strong between Outer Cove and Torbay, and the Outer Cove crew was most anxious to have another chance to beat Torbay and prove their superiority. Up until almost the last minute, there was doubt as to whether they would get the opportunity, but at last the Trademen's crew conceded the boat to the fishermen. That gave Outer Cove the chance they wanted.

There is no need to comment on how well they justified the confidence they had in themselves. The fact remains however that Outer Cove nearly lost the chance to row in that famous race of 1901 and set the record which remained unbeaten for eighty years. In that race, Torbay, rowing in the *Red Cross*, completed the course in 9:22. While this story is part of the oral history of the Regatta, it was not mentioned in the newspaper coverage of the 1901 Regatta.

SEXTON'S BRUSH WITH DEATH

By 1908, Bob Sexton was the most celebrated personality in St. John's because of his outstanding race-boat building record which included the *Blue Peter* in which the Outer Cove crew rowed the famous 9:13 record for the old course in 1901. By May of that year, he had completed a new race boat for the 1908 Regatta and had plans to rebuild a second. Then on May 31, an accident at the waterfront nearly cost him his life.

The incident occurred while Sexton was renovating the private sailing-yacht of the Honourable John Harvey. Sexton had raised the yacht at Wood's Wharf opposite Temperance Street at the east end of Water Street in St. John's. He began his work at about 4 p.m. and hoped to have it completed by nightfall. Tommy Cox, a city barber, stopped to chat with Sexton. Everyone sought Sexton's advice on the most likely boats to win at the Races. It was the era when 'betting on the races' was at its height.

Cox recalled that Sexton's five year old son Robert Des Barres Sexton (Bar) was playing on the deck. When Cox left he heard Sexton order Bar from the boat for safety reasons.

A minute or so later he heard a crushing sound and Sexton shout, "I'm killed." Turning around, Cox saw Sexton trapped under the boat which had fallen on top of him. Cox, Tom Delahunty, and Paddy Spry rushed to Sexton's aid and desperately tried to free him. The boat was too heavy, but they managed to raise it enough to relieve the tremendous pressure on Sexton. Others joined the effort and managed to raise the boat enough to pull Sexton clear.

Spry recalled that Sexton was conscious but thought he was dying. He said his features had been distorted so much that you could hardly recognize him. Sexton's face was swelled to almost twice its normal size and the features changed to the extent that those who arrived late would not believe it was Bob Sexton.

Cox noted that blood was flowing from Sexton's mouth and Sexton complained of pain in his chest. Firemen arrived on the scene and took the injured man by ambulance to the old General Hospital on Forest Road. Newspaper accounts the next day claimed that if Sexton had not been lying flat on his back and parallel to the boat, he would have been crushed to death. The accident was caused because the boat had been elevated too much without proper supports. Fortunately, Sexton had moved his position beneath the boat just seconds before the fall. The child had also managed to get off deck before the boat fell.

By July, Sexton was still hospitalized with broken ribs, a broken leg and other injuries. Yet his love for the Regatta was so strong that he insisted on being brought to lakeside to witness the launching of his new race-boat *Nina*. In those days, the launch of a new boat was an occasion for celebration. The boat was usually carried on the shoulders of rowers and escorted by a brass band to Quidi Vidi Lake.

Doctors gave in to Sexton's demands and arranged for him to be brought by ambulance to the lakeside and removed on a stretcher so he could participate in the launching of his new boat. *Nina*, however, was not the best of Sexton's boats. In its first Regatta it was outclassed by the *Blue Peter* which won eight races and had the fastest time of the day, which was 9:45.

Sexton, meanwhile, recovered from his injury and went on building boats for another forty years. His love and commitment to the Regatta and his great contribution as a boat-builder earned Bob Sexton induction into the Royal St. John's Regatta Hall of Fame.

THE REGATTA OF THE SIX BRIDES

Unusual circumstances were involved in the Regatta of 1909. Multiple weddings at Torbay combined with a visit to the Regatta by the Roman Catholic Bishop of St. John's had a unique impact on the Fishermen's Race that year.

Shortly before the 1909 Regatta, the six-rowers of the Torbay crew were all married. The Torbay crew had not won a Fishermen's Race since 1900 while the Outer Cove rowers had won five in addition to setting the 9:13 record for the old race course. The priest who performed all six weddings was pastor to Torbay and Outer Cove communities. In a pep talk to the Outer Cove crew the day before the Regatta, he acknowledged they were favoured to win. He then added a comment which left the Outer Cove crew wondering what he meant.

The priest announced that the Bishop would be at the Regatta and how nice it would be if Torbay won the Fishermen's Race. The Outer Cove men listened politely to their pastor for whom they held the highest regard. However, after he had left, they wondered aloud as to what he meant by the comment. Was he suggesting they deliberately allow Torbay to win the race? One of them recalled that the Southside crew had been barred from ever rowing in a Regatta because they fixed a race on Regatta Day, and wondered if they would be placed in the same predicament.

Finally the big day came. While the fishermen lined up at the starting buoys for the Fishermen's Race, the

Bishop, parish priest, and the six brides gathered on the north-side banks adjacent to the starting line. The big question among the few to whom the Outer Cove crew had confided their concerns was whether or not in a close contest they would hold back and allow the Torbay crew to win. In less than ten minutes all speculation ended.

The Outer Cove rowers chose to follow tradition and to row their best and let the best crew win. There was great excitement among spectators near the finish line and the six brides had tears in their eyes when the Outer Cove crew crossed the finish line first and in the time of 9:38.5.

The story of the Regatta of the six brides survived for decades and in time was embellished to the point that claims were made that the priest had actually asked the Outer Cove crew to throw the race. Regardless, it survives as one of the many colourful anecdotes of the old St. John's Regatta that help enrich its long history.

THE *BLUE PETER*

When the *Blue Peter* was lost in the CLB fire, the Royal St. John's Regatta lost its greatest treasure. The *Blue Peter* for almost 100 years was symbolic of the historic Quidi Vidi Regatta and the source of the inspirational spirit that prevailed throughout the twentieth century and kept the annual 'Day of the Races' alive.

The *Blue Peter* was a surviving material connection with the most significant race ever held on Quidi Vidi Lake; the 1901 record-setting race in which Outer Cove covered a course 160 feet longer than today's race course in just 9:13.8.

The pride of the Bob Sexton fleet of racers, the *Blue Peter* had a history on the pond that spanned the twenty-one year period from 1901 to 1922. In that time she built up a magnificent record of successes which included 165 prizes: seventy-three first prizes; sixty-one second prizes; nineteen third prizes; and twelve other awards.

Although her sister shell the *Nellie R* (another of the Sexton fleet) recorded eighty-four first place wins, she did so in a forty year period. The *Blue Peter* stands alone as the most successful racer in Regatta history. The *Blue Peter* earned its place in Regatta history at a time when the boats were not identical in size and weight and, consequently, rowers sought out the best and fastest boats on the pond.

The *Blue Peter* was designed by Dr. H. Rendell and built by Bob Sexton. Rendell designed most of the boats built by Sexton. Prior to the 1901 record setting race, the *Myrtle* (originally named the *Terra Nova*) was the fastest boat of the nineteenth century. The *Myrtle* won seven championship races between 1872 and 1900, and set the course record of 9:20 which was broken in 1901. Dr. Rendell, however, was more impressed with the design of the *Daisy*. Although the *Daisy* was a fast boat and won many races, she failed to win a championship. Yet, it was the *Daisy* upon which Dr. Rendell based his design for the famous *Blue Peter*.

When the *Blue Peter* went on the pond in 1901 a Telegram sports writer prophetically noted, "The *Blue Peter* would become the best racer ever on the pond." She was hindered in her first race and lost after being hit by the oars of the *Red Cross*. She managed to cross the finish line in second place. However, with a crew from the Star of the Sea Association in the Football-Labourer's Race, the *Blue Peter* recorded its first win at the Regatta. Later that day in the championship race, the *Blue Peter* made history by setting the 9:13.8 record which remains the record for the old course. (Official Regatta records claim that the record was broken by Smith-Stockley in 1981 with a time of 9:12.30.)

The last official Regatta Day race in which the *Blue Peter* participated was in 1922. In the championship race, the last of the day, the *Blue Peter*, manned by the Cold Storage crew, competed against Outer Cove in the *Cadet*; Logy Bay in the *Guard;* and Mixed-Trades in the *Nellie R*. That race was won by Outer Cove in the *Cadet*. It was unfortunate for Regatta history that the Outer Cove crew did not row in the *Blue Peter*. It would have been a glorious end for the boat's impressive career. Sexton had one final hand in the famous *Blue Peter* on its last day in the St. John's Regatta. During the Fishermen's Race, the *Blue Peter* was damaged. Sexton effected the repairs in one hour and she was returned to duty. She lost that race, however, to Outer Cove rowing in the *Cadet*.

Yet the *Blue Peter* was given a second chance to go out in style, although not at the St. John's Regatta. A week later hundreds lined the banks of Quidi Vidi for the Father Pippy Regatta to watch the *Blue Peter*'s last day on the pond. On August 9, 1922, the *Blue Peter*'s last run was made in the Juvenile Race with the Hussy Team rowing her against crews from St. Joseph's and St. Bon's. It proved to be a fitting conclusion to the career of the Regatta's fastest boat.

It was a closely contested race with all boats neck and neck turning the buoys and the contest remained close coming up the pond. However, in the home stretch, the *Blue Peter*'s crew, displaying a sudden surge of energy, moved the craft into a lead and then first place over the finish line.

The members of that last crew to row the *Blue Peter* were: T. Hallet, Cox; P. Taylor, stroke; G. Harvey, G. Whittle, A. Curnew, T. Cook, and F. Whitten. The *Blue Peter* was then retired to the CLB Armoury with an impressive ceremony, and remained there until destroyed by the great fire of 1992 that levelled the CLB.

The finest tribute paid to the *Blue Peter* was that given by its designer Dr. Rendell who said, "The *Blue Peter* was the best all round boat on the pond." Because of this, all

Bob Sexton's new boats were based on moulds of the *Blue Peter*. The only change made was in the shape of the bows. He did this so they could distinguish one from the other.

Although the *Blue Peter* left the pond in 1922, her influence remained for decades. By the 1950s, the 9:13 record was remembered at each Regatta. Observers offered many explanations as to why it could never be broken. Some claimed the race course had changed; others blamed the crews and some blamed the boats. In the Regatta of 1948 new boats from England were introduced to our Regatta. Times recorded by these ranged between ten and eleven minutes and people were losing interest in the Regatta.

Amid this atmosphere, the Regatta Committee of 1953 ordered new boats to replace the English-made boats. This move captured public interest when it was revealed that they would be styled after the first *Blue Peter*. The new boats were introduced into the Regatta that year and the spirit of the *Blue Peter* was revived. (Former Committee President Mike Howley studied carefully the design of the *Blue Peter* which in 1952 was still on display at the CLB Armoury, St. John's. Based on his study Mr. Howley drew up the blue prints upon which all Regatta boats since then have been built.)

NOVELTY ATTRACTIONS

Sweet scented molasses and trees near Ross's
with Fiddles playing their jigs and reels.
The pen-orth of puddin, I found much good in
around my fancy their fragrance steals.
The pole all greasy, it wasn't easy
to reach the top for the ham I'm sure,
which often hung there, by good men strung there,
at Kitty Vitty in days of yore !

(Author unknown) 1922

The side attractions at lakeside contributed to the prominent place the Regatta held in the hearts and minds of Newfoundlanders. Ron von Stein, a Regatta Committee member during the late nineteenth century, borrowed several ideas from festivals held in Germany to enrich the Quidi Vidi Regatta and stimulate interest. The most popular of these novelty attractions was the 'Greasy Pole.' This novelty, however, was used in a different form in the Regattas of the 1850s. Von Stein's version was a greased pole that extended fifty feet out into the water with prizes pinned at the end. The challenge was to walk out over the pole, retrieve a prize, and walk back without falling into the lake. The champions for several years at the Greasy Pole were Johnny Lynch and Ben Squires. Prizes included barrels of flour, two dollar cash prizes, boots, and hams. To make the novelty more challenging in 1899, it was placed upright and competitors had to climb to the top and retrieve a gift certificate. Tops at the pole that year was Alex Tapper of Torbay, Bob Lewis of St. John's, Alex Power of St. John's, and Peter Mullowney of St. John's.

Another 1850s attraction was also popular and entertaining in its day. This was the old Climbing Pole which no doubt influenced the idea for a Greasy Pole in 1896. The pole was erected upright with a height of sixty feet. Prizes were attached to the top. The challenge presented was to have the skill to climb up and retrieve a prize. This pole was not greased. It was especially popular among sailors and fishermen who were used to climbing such heights at sea.

Reference to the Climbing Pole was made in the *Times*, a St. John's newspaper, in its 1854 coverage of the Regatta. The *Times* reported, "The erection of a pole, on which from time to time was suspended at a considerable elevation with a variety of prizes, contributed to keep alive the gaiety with which the day commenced."

The Famous Dance Gallery

The Greasy Pole was the source of much memorable fun at these old time Regattas. However, it was less popular in the early twentieth century and was taken off the Regatta Program in 1912. Two factors led to its unpopularity. The first was that patrons mastered the challenge so well that the prizes were all won before noon. Even delaying the attraction by several hours failed to help. The other reason was that parents and wives complained that their men, after engaging the Greasy Pole, would come home covered in grease. An unsuccessful attempt to revise it was made in the 1970s.

THE GREASY PIG AND MORE!

Von Stein also introduced the 'Duck Hunt' and the 'Greasy Pig' attractions in 1896. Johnny Burke described the Greasy Pig attraction in his 1912 Regatta Program:

The porker was shaved as closely as Mike Murphy the barber would take the down off the upper lip of a stripling, and goodness knows, in that state would be hard enough to hold.

But to add to the difficulty of catching him he was carefully greased all over the body and legs. At a given signal he was released, and was the prize of any who could capture him. Squealing as only a pig can, he rushed through the crowds who would try to capture him. Being no respecter of persons he would bowl over men, women, and children.

He was often at liberty for hours, running through the masses of people who hemmed him in on all sides, and sometimes would escape into the lake and go on to the other side and make a break for permanent freedom; or else, being worn out from previous exertions, would find a watery grave … a fate never intended for a self-respecting 'boneen'… in the middle of the pond.

Fun on the "Greasy Pole"

Known around town as John the Baptist. Here heis attending the 1994 Regatta.

A new attraction among the concessions in 1949 was rabbit racing and it attracted large crowds. Ted Merner of Lime Street operated the traditional swinging boats at the head of the pond. It was in 1948 that the Committee began the practice of charging ground rent for concession tents. The move was not popular but it took root.

In the mid-1970s a futile attempt was made to revive the Greasy Pole and the Greasy Pig. However, modern day race fans showed more interest in racing rabbits, the Crown, and Anchor Game, the Cash Wheels and the shooting galleries. Replacing the spruce beer and crubeens (boiled pigs feet) were french fries and fish and chips. Over recent years, a new tradition is emerging that is slowly turning the one day Regatta into a two day event. Crowds today gather at lakeside on Regatta Eve and the concession-aires are beginning to respond. At around 6 p.m. Regatta Eve line-ups start forming at the Big 'R' Fish & Chip tents (one near the band-stand, the other near the boathouse). Ziggy Peel-Good also attracts crowds for their home-made french fries.

ORIENTAL PALACE

One of the most unusual attractions at lakeside was opened for the Regatta of 1893. It was the Royal Lake Pavilion, constructed by the eccentric Professor Henry Danielle of Octagon Castle fame. The Pavilion was a magnificent building that could accommodate 2,000 people in its ballroom. It was styled, furnished and decorated like a true Oriental Palace, and even included a staff of twenty-five dressed in Oriental costume. Danielle intended to conduct the Royal Lake Pavilion as a summer and winter resort. It housed a spacious and palatial ballroom which was rented out to clubs for private parties.

It also included kitchen, bedrooms, restaurant, and storerooms. The Royal opened on Saturday, August 5, and was in operation on Regatta Day, Thursday, August 10. The building was at the head of the pond a few hundred feet from the Greasy Pole. Large glass windows overlooking the pond enabled patrons to dine while watching the boat races. Hot dinners and non-alcoholic beverages only were sold at the Royal on Regatta Day. Four large stoves in a huge kitchen turned out hundreds of hot meals to Regatta Day patrons. The Oriental style palace was very popular at Regatta time, but survived only two Regattas.

CLB booth at the 1994 Regatta

The Professor had a dispute with the owner of the land whom he felt needlessly harassed the staff at the Palace. In keeping with his egocentric nature, Danielle had the Pavilion torn down, plank by plank, and the wood transported by train from Fort William to Irvene Station (near Octagon Pond) where he used the materials to build his famous Octagon Castle.

THE PLATFORM

The geographical area adjacent to and surrounding Quidi Vidi Lake was very different in the nineteenth century. Since that time banks have been levelled, hills removed, and in-filling of marshes has taken place.

Enterprising concessionaires of the era responded to the challenge by constructing platforms from which fans could watch the races from a good vantage place which was clear and dry. It was during the 1870s and 1880s that a man named Bethune, also known as a race-boat builder, constructed platforms at the head of the pond for Regatta Day. He charged forty cents admission and you could reserve an all-day seat in advance for sixty cents.

THE TOBACCO REGATTAS

During the 1930s winning crews often received tobacco along with their trophies. In 1932, the winning crew members in the Labour Race were each awarded three pounds of Black Duck Tobacco. The Truck Race winners got Bugler Tobacco while the Amateur Race winners were given a carton of cigarettes each. All tobacco was donated by the Imperial Tobacco Company. Winning crew members in the Fishermen's Race were each given a set of oil clothes and the second place winners received a side of bacon each.

WINNERS OUT!

Being a top performing crew in the first few decades of Regatta History did not get anyone into a championship race. Actually, there were no championships. If a crew won a race they were barred from competing again that day. Two races which evolved in that era were the forerunners of the championship race idea. These were the race for the Steward's Purse and the Sweepstakes Race.

THE STEWARD'S THE BOSS

The Stewards, not the Committee, held the power in the early Regattas. The Stewards made the decisions on whether the races went ahead or not. They acted as judges on the pond and enforced regulations. They started a tradition of donating prize money for the fastest boat on the pond. That race became known as the race for the Steward's Purse. The fastest boats were invited to participate, but were not obliged to do so. The Sweepstakes Race also offered top prize money. The fastest boats of the day competed in this race. All winning boats had to compete in this race or be fined twenty shillings. All boats were required to carry a twenty-two by sixteen inch flag on a staff not less than thirty inches on the gunwales of the boat.

In an effort to improve the Regatta, the Stewards introduced a regulation in 1839 restricting participation on both the four- and six-oar amateur races to residents of St. John's.

In 1844, the *Times* noted that some townspeople were upset because the Regattas were being held at Quidi Vidi, which they claimed was too far from the city. There were no boat clubs operating during the first few decades of Regatta history. The era of the boat clubs came much later and became a corner stone of the Quidi Vidi Regatta for more than half a century.

THE 1820'S ROAD

When the first Regattas were being held at Quidi Vidi Lake in the 1820s, there were two roads leading from the city to the lake. One was a military road connecting Fort William with the lake and the other was known as King's Bridge. The military road was much older and may provide support to a theory that the military rowed in competitions on the pond years earlier than the start of the Quidi Vidi Regatta. This fact, rather than a Harbour Rowing Contest, may have inspired the public Regatta at Quidi Vidi Lake.

Quidi Vidi in that era was a scenic lake outside the city limits. Boat racing was an immediate hit with city folk. The *Newfoundlander*, August 27, 1827, describes activity on that ancient road during our first Regattas. It noted, "Notwithstanding the heavy and unpromising appearance of the weather, the road leading to the lake presented, at a very early hour in the morning, unusual bustle and gaiety from the numberless gigs, wagons, and carts, all filled with happy passengers, who were jugging with joyous expectancy to the scene of amusement."

Describing the scene at lakeside, the same article stated, "As the hour for starting approached the dense heavy clouds which had lowered upon our heads were dispelled by magic influence of the blaze of beauty, elegance, and fashion which graced the borders of this beautiful sheet of water and the sun released from bondage, burst with more than wanted effulgence upon one of the most picturesque views we have ever beheld."

BREWIN'S GUN

Again I'm viewin' where once stood Brewin
the old ex-soldier who fired the gun

which set them going, a splendid showing
In my boyhood days, by the boats was done.

The famous Newfoundland song writer Johnny Burke put out a Regatta Program in 1912 with the following fascinating piece of Regatta history.

Most of us who remember the Regattas of the 1870s and 1890s will never forget a prominent figure in them. Then a venerable man in appearance, he was full of vitality, and although kindly by nature, nevertheless always to the stern discipline of the field and camp, to which he was well used.

Mr. Brewin was the man, and many of the men of today were but mere boys then. But how we watched him on the Southwest side of the pond, out on a point there on a fine day! Boys of today, and possibly many men, may not think of it. But in those days the gun was fired that one witnesses now when he sees its flash and hears its sound from Signal Hill daily. On Regatta Day, Mr. Brewin kept the fires around his gun and goodness help the boy who would tamper with it. It was a splendid sight to glance across on the head of the pond and see boats like *Lady Gover*, *Volunteer*, *Heather Belle*, and others of that type line up.

Mr. Brewin then had to be on the qui vive (lookout). No flash or shot of a moment but the poker red hot in the touch hole of the gun, ...and such a reverberation. We often held our heads in our hands as the old gentleman prepared to place the poker on the touch hole. It was a case of blazing out the fact that the races had begun, and then the same thing occurred when the boats came back. Mr. Brewin was always at his post, and the very moment the timekeeper made the motion the gun went off, and the sound went often times so far citywards as to announce that a race had been won.

And how the old gentleman would handle that gun. We boys from the East End and Maggoty Cove generally, often crowded around him while waiting between the races and never an unkind word was heard. But when the time approached for a race-stop! Mr. Brewin was there and that big gun was poised. Goodness help boy or man for that matter, that approached him. He minded nothing but the judges, and the instant the flag of the President fell out of the judge's hand, announcing the start of a race, the gun went off.

But it is today incongruous for a cannon to fire for the start and finish of a race. Mr. Brewin often saw those flashes. His grandson, James did the same. He saw heaven's artillery flashing at 11:30 p.m. one day when he jumped off a steamship in a blinding thunderstorm and saved a fellow in distress. But then, such is the world. Mr. James Brewin was the worthy grandson of a worthy grandsire.

Photo taken in 1903 from where Brewin used his cannon

The last time the ancient practice of starting the Regatta with a cannon was used was in 1897. The practice of using a starter gun began in 1898.

THE BARD OF PRESCOTT AT THE RACES

The famous Bard of Prescott Street, Johnny Burke, played a key role in the Regattas from 1871 to 1902. He began as a rower in the four-oared pilot boat called the *John*. After several years as a rower, Burke took up an active role with the Regatta Committee as a fund raiser. In those days, collectors (fund raisers) were assigned to geographical areas of the city to canvass all business places in the given area for donations. Burke was considered very effective in his efforts. He served in various capacities with the Committee during the 1890s. In 1902, his opposition to the sale of alcohol at the Regatta led to his resignation.

Burke was also critical of Regatta Day luncheons. In those days the races came to a complete stop when the Committee broke for lunch. Often the Committee left the lake to have lunch in nearby dining halls. Frequently they were late returning. This practice angered the rowers and Burke felt housewives were also disadvantaged by it. He said the women would wait until after lunch to visit the Regatta and if the races were delayed too long due to the luncheon they would leave the Regatta. Many people, including the rowers, argued that the dinners should be held after Regatta Day.

THE BOUNCE BOAT RACES

A peculiar oddity of the Quidi Vidi Regatta was the nineteenth century Bounce Boat Races. Bounce Boat (also called Bouncer Boats) racing was a popular attraction of the late 1880s and early 1890s. The man responsible for the creation of the Bouncer Boat was Robert Sexton. Sexton is the famous Regatta Hall of Fame member who built some of the best race boats ever put on Quidi Vidi.

Sexton began his association with the Regatta, not as a boat builder, but as a participant in the yacht races. Yacht races were part of the first Regattas. During the first twenty-five years of Regatta history, these races were held on the second day of the annual Regatta and took place on St. John's Harbour. Actually, these yachts were large sailing boats.

Sexton, acclaimed for his boat building genius, saw a way to improve the speed of yachts on the pond. He designed a sail boat similar in design to the large ones but reduced the size and weight. The miniature sail boat outclassed the others and in no time there were six in competition on Quidi Vidi Lake. They were dubbed the Bounce Boats because of the way they bounced over the waves at Quidi Vidi.

In the Regatta of 1893, there were six bouncer boats and the Regatta Committee offered a silver cup for the winner of the special Bounce Boat Race. The course for these races was twice up and down the pond. Sexton teamed up with Dr. H. Rendell in the *Bob Tail* and took first prize. Sexton's own boat, the *Trilby*, called after the girlfriend of a prominent city bachelor, was barred from competition. Officials disqualified the *Trilby* because Sexton had installed foot rests in the boat. He did take the boat around the pond to test its speed before being forced to tie her up.

The Bouncer Boat was described in the *Telegram* of 1893 as, "A class of small but fast and efficient sail boat." The Bouncer's had colourful names like the *Jim Jam, Wig Wag,* and the *Pirate*.

Sexton and Rendell often competed as a team in the Bounce Boat Races. The duo became a powerful force in Regatta history when they joined in building some of the best boats ever to compete in Regatta competition.

Rendell designed many of the boats constructed by Bob Sexton.

THE VICTORIA CARRIAGE

The Committee's Victoria Carriage was as familiar at lakeside as the race boats themselves. The Committee used to hire a local carriage and driver to carry the Regatta judges up and down the north bank as they followed each race. Two of the regular cabmen for years were Mr. J. Dodd and Matt Kelly.

The last Victoria Carriage to be hired was owned by George Symonds of St. John's. When he passed away in 1953, the Committee purchased the Victoria at a price of 100 dollars.

Traditionally, the Victoria picked up the Committee President, Vice President, and Secretary and took them to lakeside in time for the first race of the day. The caretaker at Bowring Park always had fresh roses to pin in the lapels of Committee members once the go-ahead was given for the Regatta.

GENEROUS BUILDER

Sam Loveys, the greatest race-boat builder of the nineteenth century Regattas, was so pleased over the outcome of a race at the 1855 Regatta that he gave away one of his best built race-boats. Loveys, who introduced the race-shell boats to the Regatta in 1844, put a new boat on the pond in 1855 which inspired a great deal of speculation and lakeside gambling. The boat, which he christened the *Darling*, was scheduled to compete against the *Undeen*, another Loveys boat which he built for the 1854 Regatta.

Speculation over which was the faster boat dominated conversation among spectators and a fifty-pound English Sterling prize was offered for the winning boat. Loveys agreed to the match and the competition between the *Darling,* rowed by a Quidi Vidi crew, and the *Undeen,* rowed by a St. John's crew, became a highlight of that year's Regatta. The race was close going down the pond but after turning the buoys, the *Darling* took a comfortable lead and kept it to the finish. Lovey's, who had claimed that the *Darling* was the superior boat prior to Regatta Day, was so pleased by the outcome that he made a gift of the winning boat to the Quidi Vidi rowing crew.

SILVER CUPS

Prior to 1872, cash prizes were awarded to winning crews on Regatta Day. However the year 1879 marked the first time in history that a silver cup trophy was awarded. George E. Wilson, promoting a play he was directing in St. John's, offered several Regatta Day prizes to get publicity for his show. He donated two silver cups; one for the four-oared Amateur Race winners and the other for the six-oared Amateur Race winners. A Tea Urn was the prize he donated for the six-oared Fishermen's Race. Outer Cove, rowing in the *Elizabeth,* won the Fishermen's Race that year.

US MILITARY AIDS REGATTA

The United States Air Force (USAF) came to the aid of the Regatta in 1943 when, because of the shortage of materials due to the war, the Committee was unable to obtain trophies on the local market. Major-General

Brock of the US Army contacted the USAF in Washington with an urgent request to fly in trophies to St. John's in time for Regatta Day. The trophies arrived on schedule and became instantly popular among competitors. The trophy depicted the figure of an oarsman finished in gold and silver. Many rowers who won cash prizes offered to exchange the cash for the American-made trophies.

AN AMERICAN FIRST

In 1954, for the first time in Regatta history, an American crew won the Regatta Championship. American participation in the Regatta spanned the years from 1945 to 1957. By 1958, the Americans had pulled out of Pleasantville leaving only a skeleton staff to care for the property until Canadian authorities assumed ownership. This was also the first year since 1945 that a US Armed Forces Band did not play at lakeside on Regatta Day. Another notable event this year was the official opening of the Higgins Memorial on the north side of the pond.

RELIGION AT THE REGATTA

In the 1930s and 1940s, religion played a role in the selection of Regatta Committee Presidents. According to John Perlin, a former Committee President and an inductee into the Regatta Hall of Fame, "In those days a Roman Catholic President served in that office as long as he wanted to and it was only with the death and retirement of Mr. Justice Jim Higgins that the current two year presidential term was initiated. It was during Gerry

Angel's term that changes began to be made in the executive office."

Perlin went on to explain the growth of the Committee. He said it was once, "...a parochial, self perpetuating, anachronistic, archaic community event to one that has become international in its scope and is attracting more young participants than ever before. It is also a big business that requires professional management to ensure its continuing success and future well being."

When the Regatta Committee was incorporated in 1936, its first objective was to encourage aquatic sports of all kinds and not just rowing.

FIRST BROADCAST OF THE REGATTA

The first radio broadcast of a St. John's Regatta took place in 1938. The announcer was Bill Galgay who used the on-air name Frank Barclay. The event was the work of the Dominion Broadcasting Company. Galgay was not content to broadcast from shore. He was anxious for all listeners to hear the shouts of the coxswains, the splash of oars, and the excitement at the turning of the buoys. He and his technicians built the first mobile transmitter in a cigar box which they used to better report on the races on the pond.

CHAPTER TWO

Regatta Humour

We placed afloat the new race boat
just as the sun was setting
and Mr. Reid, we think he need
have no cause for regretting.
While six good men got in her then
as silenced reigned unbroken
Till Mrs. Reid in word and deed
performed the ancient token.

The Launch of the *Red Lion*
by Jimmy Murphy, 1906

REGATTA JUSTICE

Throughout the long history of the Regatta many humourous and witty incidents took place. One funny episode took place about a month after the 1921 Regatta in the old court house building at St. John's and actually made Newfoundland justice history. For the first and only time in criminal history, the defence blamed a crime on the Regatta.

The case involved an altercation between a married couple known by their neighbours as Charlie and Aunt Liz in their home on Cuddihy Street (now occupied by St. John's City Hall). The judge was Judge Morris and the defendant's lawyer was G.W.B. Ayre. Charlie was charged with assaulting his wife.

Neighbours of the two knew all too well that poor Charlie was a henpecked husband who never had the courage to speak back let alone strike his missus. But somehow, several days after the Regatta, he summoned the courage to challenge Aunt Liz's authority and to strike back. Charlie had a wonderful day at the Regatta and, for several days after, had visited one of the Water Street shebeens (bootlegging establishments) where he purchased illegal liquor. To hide their activities from police, the operators filled vanilla bottles with rum and placed them on a high shelf behind the counter. Thirsty customers would drop buy to pick up their supply of so-called vanilla extract which sold for ten cents a bottle.

Soon after arriving home from a shebeen visit, Charlie began singing every Irish ditty he knew at the top of his lungs. Although neighbours often challenged Charlie to stand up to his wife, he could never summon the courage to do so. But this week he was really walking a thin line at home.

When Aunt Liz decided that 'enough was enough' and ordered Charlie to 'hold his mouth,' Charlie totally ignored her. As a matter of fact, Charlie had gotten enough courage from the vanilla bottle that he decided to rebel.

Liz, feeling that she had put up with enough, told Charlie she was going for the 'Black Mariah' (police wagon) to have him locked up. But before she could get to the door, Charlie picked up his cane and gave her a couple of wacks on the rear end. This put the devil in Liz and she was determined to settle for nothing less than having Charlie brought before the judge. Not long after, the police came and Liz signed the complaint to have Charlie arrested.

When Charlie's lawyer, G.W.B. Ayre, was made aware of the facts, he decided to base his defence on the fact that Charlie had attended the Regatta and had gotten caught up in the Regatta spirit. In court, Mr. Ayre argued that Charlie, by all accounts, was not a violent man and his behaviour on the occasion of the assault was out of the ordinary. He summed up his defence in one sentence, "My client had been on a good time at the Regatta and had not recovered yet."

Although a big Regatta fan himself, Judge Morris was not impressed with the argument. He strongly criticized Charlie's behaviour and, "bound him over to keep the peace in a personal bond of $200 and two sureties of $100 each."

THE GULL AND MRS. REID

In 1906, Reid Newfoundland Limited had a new boat built by Bob Sexton for that year's Regatta. The launching of a new Sexton-built race boat was always an occasion for celebration and this was no exception. A Scottish pipe band escorted by mounted police, '...played the boat down to the lake,' where the most prominent people of St. John's society had gathered. Mrs. Reid was given the honour of christening the new boat with the name *Lion*.

Spectators lined the banks to watch the ceremony. Among them a character from town known as 'The Gull' clinched a near empty bottle of home-brew. Following the introductions and round of speeches, Mrs. Reid was passed the traditional bottle of champagne to christen the boat. She gently stepped forward and swung the bottle hitting the boat's bow. But nothing happened. The bottle didn't break and the crowds withheld the traditional three cheers. A little embarrassed, Mrs. Reid again swung the bottle. The Gull, wide eyed and clutching his near empty bottle, was the only one to shout 'Hurrah!' when for the second time the bottle didn't break.

Mrs. Reid, by now a little frustrated, made a third attempt. A whisper went through the crowd when the champagne bottle again failed to break. Mrs. Reid was no longer ready to leave the christening to chance so she grabbed a nearby hammer and smashed the bottle of champagne. As the champagne was tossed over the new boat the traditional three cheers from the banks broke out. The only one not smiling at the turn of events was The Gull who finished off his home-brew and left the pond disgusted. Friends said The Gull always lamented the waste of champagne for such events.

THREE STOOGES' DAY AT THE RACES

The year 1936 was an historic day in the history of the Regatta. In that year, Quidi Vidi Lake area was made a National Park and named King George's Park. Yet for decades, townspeople remembered the day for an episode that occurred near the finish line in the Fishermen's Race.

There was heavy betting at lakeside on the Fishermen's Race with Torbay and Outer Cove the favoured teams. The two crews were neck and neck nearing the finish line when an Outer Cove fan, feeling the effects of, "...tipping too much of the National" (excessive drinking) waded into the water and tried to swim out to the boats. Not to be outdone, a Torbay man, feeling equally as daring, went after him. He too had been 'tipping the National' and had forgotten that he couldn't swim. When the water came up to his neck he suddenly realized the dangerous predicament he was putting himself in and stopped. Just as he was turning to head back to shore, a Blackhead fan ran out in long-rubbers to help but collided with the Torbay man and two of them went under. Meanwhile, the Outer Cove man had heard the shouting from the banks and, seeing the two in trouble, swam to their aid. The two managed to get a footing when the Outer Cove man came charging in and knocked the two back under water. The three then pooled their efforts and helped each other back to the banks and safety. A tragedy was averted. The Torbay crew won the race but Torbay came close to losing a fan.

REGATTA MOTTO

During the 1880s the Regatta's motto was "Be temperate, genial, and happy." The motto was part of an effort to discourage excessive drinking and encourage people to enjoy the day at the races. During the Regatta of 1885, Paddy Murphy, having had far too much to drink, decided to swim across Quidi Vidi Lake. When Murphy, attired in coveralls and a salt-and-pepper hat, waded into the lake, the boats were just leaving the starting line. Constabulary Corporal Tim Dooley, in full uniform, dove in after Murphy and succeeded in dragging him back to shore. Nearby spectators gave the Constable a round of applause. Looking at Murphy in a horizontal position on the ground a lady nearby commented to Dooley, "And the Regatta's motto is, 'be temperate, genial and happy.'" To which Dooley quipped, "Well, two out of three is not bad for Murphy."

THE GAMBLER

In 1894, Billy Connors worked as a labourer on the docks (Harbour front). Billy was a gambler who loved Regatta Day. In 1894, he went to the Regatta with two dollars in his pocket (a week's wages) convinced that by day's end he would accumulate eight to ten dollars in winnings. Like other Regatta Day gamblers, Billy was down at lakeside every night watching the practices and getting to know the best boats on the pond.

He was doing well on Regatta Day and by mid-afternoon had won twenty dollars. Although he had surpassed his own expectations he was convinced he was on a winning streak. He told friends he had a good feeling about the *Lilly* because she had done well in practice that week. Despite the urging from friends to keep his winnings, Billy bet the entire twenty dollars on the *Lilly*. But his luck had run out. The *Lilly* came in third and Billy was now broke, and a sore loser.

He was determined to wreck revenge on the *Lilly* and waited around the lake until night fall. When everyone had left the lake, he broke into the boathouse where the *Lilly* was stored and began kicking the boat indiscriminately. When he had finished there were several holes in the boat, but poor Bill had broken an ankle during the venting of his rage. He was now faced with the problem of getting back to town on a crippled and painful foot.

Billy made a crutch from wood taken from a nearby tree and hopped his way back to St. John's empty handed and cursing all the way.

CAPTAIN HORSE
AND THE JINX MARINES

Richard Squires earned a place in Regatta history by winning a highly anticipated challenge race against the Nova Scotia Scull Champion, George Ferguson. Ferguson had won the Scull Race on Regatta Day and his backers (Nova Scotian sea-captains in port) picked up the winning cash-pot. The win was criticized by local spectators who argued that Ferguson had an unfair advantage in the race. The St. John's rowers were forced to row a back-to-back set of races. While they had no time to rest, Ferguson had all afternoon. He angered the city population even more when he told reporters, "...some in the city are just poor losers."

The pride of Newfoundlanders was hurt and Richard Squires, a well-known and powerful sculler from St. Phillips, issued a public challenge to Ferguson which was accepted. The race was set for Saturday, August 22 at 2 p.m. City fans eagerly looked forward to the race and the chance to regain, "...our national pride." Once more the Nova Scotia captains put up a lot of money on their man. Crowds turned up at lakeside to witness the spectacle and cheer on their man...Richard Squires. Squires quickly established his superiority and was in so far a lead that Ferguson rowed to shore and gave up the race. Now it was local fans time to gloat.

A tongue-in-cheek letter to the newspapers claimed an Outer Cove woman was about to challenge Ferguson for a 1,000 dollar purse. The writer suggested the band at lakeside serenade Ferguson with some of the novelty songs of the time: *Captain Horse and the Jinx Marines*; *I Couldn't Help Laughing*; *How far is that for I*; and *Wait for the Tide to Turn*. (More detailed story of the Squires-Ferguson Race is told in Chapter Nine.)

TOADS, RATTLESNAKES
AND POLITICIANS

Toads and rattlesnakes were among the novelties at the 1883 Regatta. Newspaper editors took shots at each other whenever the opportunity arose. In that year the *Evening Telegram,* reporting on the strange side show, used the opportunity to attack the *Evening Mercury* and the politicians of the day by stating:

> The exhibition of rattlesnakes and Nova Scotian toads for tomorrow on the Regatta Grounds at Quidi Vidi ought, of course, to embrace the reverend reptile of the Ting's *Evening Mercury* and the newly imported parasite who crawls about town in quest of editorial pablum for the editor-in-chief. Perhaps they will be there! Who knows? But after all, few persons if any will care to pay for the privilege of seeing a toad when almost every public office in the country contains one or more of these animals.

KEEP OFF THE GRASS

It made perfect sense in 1902 and people took it serious. However, 100 years later the warning signs on the north bank of Quidi Vidi placed there for the 1902 Regatta will no doubt draw a chuckle from any reader.

In that era there were farms on the north side of the pond and cattle watered at the lake and grazed along its banks. On Regatta Day, farmers cooperated by keeping their cattle from interfering. The warnings reminded the public, "...not to sit on the grass near lakeside with frock coats because the cattle were grazing there last night."

There was no permanent band stand. Each year a temporary wooden one was erected near the Committee tent. At the end of the Regatta, thieves sometimes stole the wood used to build the stand. This prompted J.J. Callahan, whose firm erected the stands, to warn would-be thieves, "Don't touch the boards, lest you be given free board on the other side of the lake."

Fans enjoying a day at the races 1957. Kathleen Kavanagh (a familiar St. John's resident from Flower Hill) is at far left. Photo courtesy of the Provincial Archives of Newfoundland and Labrador.

One practice that remains the same as 100 years ago is that of spectators on the bank trying to tell coxswains how to do their job. An observant reporter warned fans, "...don't tell the cox anything about the different necessary cuts....else you might get a few by way of illustration." Someone commented that A. Williams, cox of the

Blackhead crew, "...had so many medals he was gold-plated." But nobody tried to tell Williams how to do his job. His Blackhead crew was second in eighty years only to the 1901 Outer Cove crew.

OUR PRESIDENT

In 1907, the Catholic Cadet Corps was treated to a banquet at Woods West End Restaurant (corner of Water and Holdsworth Streets). The dinner was given to honour the crew for winning the Brigade Race over the CLB and the Methodist Brigade. Woods served an impressive menu: oxen soup; choice of roast goose and apple sauce or lamb and mint sauce; potatoes, peas, stewed tomatoes; and for dessert an apricot tart. As the evening went on, numerous toasts were made. The audience was a little taken back when a Mr. Cohen proposed a toast to President Teddy Roosevelt. But they joined in when Cohen led them in singing *For He's a Jolly Good Fellow*.

TORBAY SHOW

Torbay pulled an upset in the Fishermen's Race of 1910 by defeating crews from Outer Cove, Bell Island, and Flatrock. Outer Cove was favoured to win but Torbay finished first in a time of 9:36.6. For several years, crews refused to row in a championship because by that race the cash award for the fastest time of the day was already won; 1910 was such a year. Invigorated by their upset, the Torbay crew arranged to row alone after the last race in an effort to beat Outer Cove's 1901 record. The challenge to the record inspired thousands to remain at lakeside for the event. While Torbay fans cheered their rowers on, the Outer Cove crew jeered and shouted insults to the rowers. One cry was, "Hurry up, winter's coming and ye'll be stuck on the ice." Outer Cove was delighted when it was announced that Torbay recorded 9:35 in that race. Far short of the record.

HARD TIMES

Inflation over the war years carried into 1920. The old custom of serving liquor at the Committee tent was dropped and there was plenty of bologna and sausages sold at tents on both sides of the lake. Sugar prices had jumped days before the Regatta which prompted one reporter to comment, "If there was a boat on the pond called 'The Price of Sugar,' I'd bet my last dollar on her after she turned the buoy."

PONDSIDE WIT

On the eve of the 1921 Regatta a delivery man named Billy Cunningham was trying to wash his horse in the lake when she went out over her head. Cunningham was on the horse's back and tried hard to save her. While some men on the banks tried to help, a labourer quipped: "The Captain only goes down with his ship." All rescue efforts failed and the horse drowned.

WAR GAMES

The Swinging Boats, Wheel of Fortune, and a game called Spill the Milk were popular at the 1940s' Regattas but not as popular as two games at lakeside that had been inspired by the war. Although the two tents were not close to each other they had the same theme. One was called "Hit The Jap" and the other "Hit Hirohito." In both, a local lad dressed as a Japanese soldier with his head protruding through a hole in the wall would bob up and down, left and right, to avoid being hit by a ball. Patrons got three tries for ten cents and if they hit the 'Jap' or 'Hirohito' they won the prize.

OLD BENEDICTS

In 1945, the Regatta Committee refused a request to include a ladies race in the Victory Regatta. One lady was angered enough to pen a letter to the *Telegram* taking the Committee to task for the decision. She wrote (referring to Committee members), "How soon you old Benedicts forget your courting days and the promises you all made sometime or another to some fair damsel." Gert Reardigan, an honoured member of the Regatta Hall of Fame denies having anything to do with the letter. In 1949, Gert persuaded the Committee to include a ladies race in the Regatta program. It marked the first time in history that ladies were included in a Regatta Day program. In 1856, a ladies crew from Quidi Vidi rowed in a Bye-Race held days after the Regatta program had been completed.

WET PAINT

At old-time Regattas, the Committee members turned up at lakeside in their Sunday-go-meeting clothes. Aubrey McDonald, better known as Aubrey Mack, was broadcasting the races. Mack had a sharp eye for funny situations and a wit to match. Lew Crane, serving as time keeper that year, sat on wet paint in the judges' boat and spoiled his new suit. Mack told listeners, "The judges' boat had a new coat of paint but the paint did not take kindly at all to Lew Crane's brand new suit. Lew is a great fellow at timing boats...but not so good at taking the time it takes for paint to dry."

Mack in describing the ladies at the lake commented, "The ladies look very attractive here today. Some in white dresses of many colours and some with no colours at all."

POOR ROWER

During the mid-1920s, the Benevolent Irish Society (BIS) crew found themselves on the horns of a dilemma. There was a weak man in the boat, but the other crew members didn't have the heart to tell him. As Regatta Day drew near, the coxswain decided that he would take the bull by the horns and confront the weak man. He told the others, "We'll have to throw sentiment aside and tell Jim that he'll have to be replaced."

The next day at practice, the cox called Jim aside and reluctantly said, "I don't know if you know it, but there's a weak man in the boat, and..." that's as far as he got. Jim replied excitedly, "That's alright," bubbling over with enthusiasm and confidence, "tell you what you'll do...you just add a few more inches to my oar, and I'll make up for the weak man!"

HONOURABLE SOAKING

During the 1920s, it was traditional for a few Committee members to be assigned the task of firing the gun to start each race. They would usually take every third or fourth race so each man could have some time to enjoy the day. On one occasion at about 5 p.m.

one of the starters had been having a drop of the 'national' and fell asleep. Suddenly someone shouted, "Time for the next race!" The judges' boat was already at the head of the pond but our friend, hearing the shout, jumped to his feet and ran madly down the wharf, jumped into the boat, but there was no boat there. Friends pulled the embarrassed fellow from the pond and the race went ahead on schedule; without him.

THE COW

During one of the Regattas of the late 1930s, a new coxswain on the pond was very keen but lacking in experience. He looked the part of a coxswain, being short and light, but he had very little knowledge of the technique of taking a crew down the pond and back.

Several days before the races, he asked a fellow cox for some advice. The old-timer asked, "What buoy are you on?" On being told the stake and buoy the adviser said, "It's quite simple. After you get below the boathouse, steer for the white house at the foot of the pond. That's right in line with the buoy you've drawn. You can't go wrong." The newcomer was delighted and expressed his thanks to the veteran.

On Regatta Day, his crew got off to a great start and was in the race all the way. Mindful of his instructions, he kept his eyes fixed on the white house and paid little attention to getting to his buoy.

Unfortunately, when he got to the foot of the pond, he discovered to his horror that he was heading for the wrong buoy. In his excitement he had picked as his guiding point not the white house but a white cow which was grazing in the field at the foot of the lake. His crew came in last and our hero nearly ended up in Belvedere (cemetery).

LOST ON THE POND

The year 1945 was dubbed the Victory Regatta to honour the ending of World War II. There were larger crowds than usual and hop-beer tents were popular among the military as well as the locals. The US Army had provided a rescue boat during the 1940s and in 1945, the boat was involved in a comic scene on the pond.

The *Coronet* crashed into the *Star of the Sea* boat shearing off a section of the stern and dumping the *Star*'s rowers into the pond. The rescue boat rushed to the scene and was applauded when they pulled the embarrassed *Star* rowers from the pond. With the crowd cheering and all eyes on the rescue boat it proceeded to take the rowers to safety. However, they landed them on the wrong side of the pond; the north side. The *Star of the Sea* boathouse was on the south side. The Americans were good sports and did not hesitate to correct the mistake and took the rowers to their own boathouse. Interest in the Regatta began to increase after the war and in 1946, the four-oared races were dropped from the program.

DUM DA DIDDLEY

This Regatta anthem along with its popular names, *Banks Of Newfoundland* and *Up The Pond*, was also known as *Dum Da Diddley* (because the tune had no words, fans would sing along with the music repeating 'Dum Da Diddley'). For more than half a century the famous *Banks of Newfoundland* was considered the national anthem of Newfoundland. Even when the *Ode to Newfoundland* was introduced in 1902, and for two decades afterwards, people still honoured *Up the Pond* and would come to attention whenever it was played at a public function.

Although the *Ode to Newfoundland* has replaced the *Banks of Newfoundland* as our anthem, the tune is as popular today as it ever was, and has become synonymous with the St. John's Regatta. The music was written by Sir Francis Forbes, Chief Justice of Newfoundland during the early nineteenth century. Forbes wrote the tune in 1820 while passing away time on the Grand Banks when his ship was lost in fog.

An indication of its popularity is reflected in the words of Sir Edward Morris as printed in the *Daily News* of May 23, 1929: "How surprised would have been Sir Francis Forbes, could he have looked into the future, to find this composition being played before royalty, and at the parade of the Lord Mayor of London, in France and in Scotland, the old home of the Forbes family."

Forbes was born in Bermuda to Scottish parents and was educated in England. He was appointed Chief Justice of Newfoundland in 1816, and sworn in on July 15, 1817. Failing health forced him to move to England in 1822. He passed away at Leitrim near Sydney, Australia, on November 9, 1841.

CHAPTER THREE

Sooks of the Regatta

*We have our faults perhaps, slight ones if
any.
We have our virtues, big, middling and
small.
We have our differences — not very many
But soon they'll be fewer — thus pray*

OARSMEN ALL
by Mary Ellen Spry

NO PHIL BROWN — NO RACE

Participants of the St. John's Regattas were not always good sports. Many times throughout Regatta history crews were down right sooks. In 1925 the Outer Cove crew raised eyebrows by absolutely refusing to row in the championship race. The reason: their cox, Phil Brown, had chosen to go with the Torbay crew in the championship race. Outer Cove, with Phil Brown as their cox, had defeated crews from the Battery, Torbay and Blackhead. Their time was 9:48. Although a top cox was available to the Outer Cove six, they turned their backs and went home. Consequently, only two crews competed in the 1925 Regatta Championship Torbay and Breen's Trucking. Because of the controversy, Brown did not go with Torbay. Instead, R. Codner took the crew. The race was won by Torbay in the time of 9:48.8. Less than a second's difference from the Outer Cove team.

TORBAY'S TURN

A year later in 1926, it was Torbay's turn to sook. Outer Cove barely edged out the Torbay crew with a time of 9:50.4 in the Fishermen's Race. The anger of the Torbay crew and their fans was soon evident all over the course. Torbay loudly protested that they were cheated out of the win. They claimed they were distracted when Sir John Crosbie accidentally fired the starter-gun just before the race ended. The gun-fire, claimed Torbay, distracted them long enough for Outer Cove to get the edge. Sir John tried to calm the atmosphere by suggesting a rematch and offering 250 dollars to the winners. The Blue Peter Boat Club offered an additional fifty-dollars. Obviously, the win meant more to Outer Cove than the possibility of a 300 dollar purse in a rematch and they refused to row again. Sir John had to be escorted from the pond for his own protection.

In 1935, there was another angry Torbay crew at the Regatta. They were fuming because the Committee would not allow them to row in the *Nellie R* for the Championship Race. At that Regatta the Fishermen's Race had to be cancelled when Hueston, of Outer Cove, sprained his arm and no substitute was available. Torbay was given the privilege of rowing for time. They covered the course in 9:52 in the *Nellie R*. They earned a spot in the Championship Race but flatly refused to participate because they were not assigned the *Nellie R*. The West End Police were assigned the famous *Nellie R* and won the championship with a time of 9:47.

In order to entice the fishermen to row in the 1935 Regatta, the Committee had to provide transportation to and from the course for the rowers and toss in a case of lubricating oil to the winners as an incentive.

BLACKHEAD

Championship races were not always part of Regatta Day. The crew with the fastest time would get a cash bonus along with their prize. Because the Championship Race did not offer money, rowers were not inclined to wait around until the end of the day to compete. Although a Championship Race was scheduled for the 1906 Regatta, the crews that qualified to participate refused to row. Included in that group of 'sports' was the Blackhead crew which won the Fishermen's Race in the time of 9:34; the best for the day. An amateur crew had a time of 9:40. The Reid Newfoundland crew with a time of 10:07 and the Southside Firemen's crew and a Tradesmen's crew, each with a time of 10:10. All refused to row in a championship race and chose instead to leave the course early. Blackhead had won the Fishermen's Race and the championship Race in 1904 and 1905. They won the 1904 Fishermen's Race in a time of 9:21.8, which remains the second best time on the old course.

THE *NATIVE*

While the St. John's Regatta was always immensely popular, there were times when public clashes and rowers' anger distracted attention from the positive aspects of the People's Day.

An outrageous incident took place during the Regatta of 1881. That year a strapping young crew from Torbay rowed the *Native*, a handsome boat of the day. They were favourites by huge odds to sweep all honours at the races.

View at the annual St. John's Regatta early 1900s. Photo courtesy of the Provincial Archives of Newfoundland and Labrador.

It seemed that there was some fault with the boat rather than the rowers. Throughout the day several good crews manned the *Native* but could do no better than third or fourth place. Gamblers at pondside lost a lot of money on the *Native*. When the Torbay crew rowing in the *Native* were soundly beaten in the six-oared event, they found revenge in the afternoon four-oared set race (Fishermen's Race).

Though their oarsmanship was perfect, they were badly beaten a second time. Humiliated by the double defeat, the crew did not stop after passing the finishing line. To the amazement of fans, the Torbay crew continued to row and beached the boat high and dry at the head of the pond. Fans were even more startled when they watched the crew jump up and down in the boat until the bottom burst open. They followed this with kicking at the sides until the *Native* was wrecked so badly that the owners were never able to repair her.

ANGRY OUTER COVE

The people of St. John's were delighted to see the Regatta revived in 1871, after a ten year absence. The day of celebration, however, was not without controversy. A newspaper report of the cup winners on Regatta Day neglected to name the individual crew members of the Outer Cove crew. This omission sparked public controversy.

In 1871 for the first time in Regatta history, silver cups were offered as prizes instead of money. The silver cups were donated by George Wilson, owner of a theatre group performing in St. John's that summer. The presentation of awards was made just before the presentation of Wilson's play the "Little Detective."

A series of letters to the *Newfoundland Chronicle* accused the newspaper of putting down Newfoundland fishermen. One letter stated,

> If any men were entitled to have their names published in connection with this matter, it should be these, for this very reason alone. Besides, they rowed

against men, not boys, opponents who were worthy of
their steel. Signed...Honour to whom Honour is Due.

The *Chronicle* defended its omission and claimed
their reporter had unsuccessfully sought to get the
names of the Outer Cove crew after the races on Regatta
Day. The editor apologized to the Outer Cove crew and
said, "...no offence was intended." The names were published along with the apology.

TARGETED COMMITTEE MEMBER

Public anger was also directed at John E. Roach, cox of
the winning boat, *The Lady of the Lake*. Rowers accused
Roach of showing favouritism by bringing his crew into
the Committee tent for refreshments. Other rowers
showered verbal abuse on Roach and on the crew for
accepting the invitation.

Another angry episode took place at the 1871
Regatta. Most races that day were so closely contested
that spectators didn't know who won. Such was the case
in the Amateur Race; the first of the day. This race was
won by the *John*, a fast race boat that year. However, minutes after the race, the crew was disqualified and the second place crew was awarded first place. The disqualifi-
cation followed disclosure to the Committee that one of
the *John* crew members had not registered before the
race.

One writer to the press declared,

> There is a rule, that recognizes in all such trials of
> skill as boat racing is, as stated, that whatever objec-
> tions there may be to any of the competition should be
> made previous to the contest and not after. The very

fact a place was allotted to her in the race, entitled these young men to their well earned laurels.

The Committee remained steadfast in their decision.

THE CLAPP TRAP

In 1875, the All-Comers Race was introduced to the Regatta. First place went to the Joiners (Tradesmen Division) in the *Mary*. A cash prize was awarded which the crew and cox shared. Bad feelings had developed between G.T. Clapp, cox, and the crew. Clapp was looked upon as a greedy person and the crew contrived an incident to draw public attention to this in order to embarrass him publicly.

Without telling Clapp, the crew donated their winnings to the boat club which owned the *Volunteer* for their boat fund. Mr. J.W. Greenway, club chairman, issued a public statement acknowledging the generosity of the crew and noted that Clapp did not contribute his share.

An indignant Clapp responded in the *Chronicle* on August 17, 1875, stating, "I can only say J.W. Greenway knowingly and maliciously insinuated what was false." Clapp said he was unaware of his crew's intention to donate to the boat account and if he had known he would have gladly joined the move. He concluded, "I shall not allow Mr. Greenway's malice to prevent my now tendering you the sum of my share of winnings in the six oar race." The crew and their friends had a great laugh and felt they had squeezed the money out of their greedy cox and in doing so had embarrassed him. The crew never again used Clapp as their cox.

FIXED RACE

A scandal marred the Regatta of 1886. The Southside Tradesmen won the six-oared race but lost the four-oared race while rowing in the *Resolute*. That night, while celebrating their victory, one of the rowers told supporters how they had made more money by deliberately losing the race than if they had won. He explained they had agreed to throw the race and actually bet money on their opponents. Word of the 'fix' reached members of the Committee and a special meeting was convened.

The Committee banned the Southside crew from ever rowing on the pond again. At the Regatta of 1894, two of the outlawed rowers registered to row in the *Daisy*. When the Committee learned of their registration, they read the banning law of 1886 and disallowed the two from any participation in the races. This was the only time in the history of the Regatta that a law was passed to ban individual rowers from participation.

SABOTAGE

During the 1830s and 1840s some of the fastest boats on the pond were imported from Halifax. This hurt the pride of many fans who viewed the importation of foreign boats as an insult to our native boat builders.

This resentment led to a major act of vandalism during the Regatta of 1840. A local merchant had housed his Halifax-built boat the *Victoria,* in a large tent at lakeside. On the night before the Regatta, the tent and the boat came under attack. The vandals cut the tent into ribbons and hammered holes in the bow of the *Victoria*. When they left, they took the boat's oars with them. The *Victoria* was scheduled to be rowed Regatta Day by a crew from Quidi Vidi in competition against the Pilots in a locally built boat.

When the scheduled time arrived, the Pilots were at the starting point with no sign of the *Victoria*. A local boat builder had been called to repair the *Victoria* and had been working all morning to meet the deadline for the race. Meanwhile, the Pilots insisted that they be allowed to row the course alone, in accordance with the rules, and claim the cash prize for first place. They did so and gleefully accepted the honours.

But just as they passed the finish line, the Quidi Vidi crew rowed the *Victoria* to the starting place and sought to have the race rescheduled. A shouting match followed among the rowers and Committee members. To entice the Pilots to agree to the contest, one merchant offered a twenty-pound cash prize. However, the Pilots were satisfied with winning by default and flatly refused to compete. They claimed the prize money was legally theirs. Fans who resented the Halifax boats cheered the decision. Although it was never proven, it was believed that members of the Pilots' crew had sabotaged the Halifax build...as an act of patriotism.

BRAWL

There were fights galore at the old time Regattas. During the 1930s, a near riot broke out when patrons of a hop-beer tent caught the operator going to and from the pond to fetch water which he used to water down the beer. Another story tells how an American seaman challenged all and sundry and defeated each opponent by a knockout until he ran up against one Bradbury from Torbay.

The latter was a giant of a man and he quickly disposed of his adversary. Sometimes disputes over favourite race boats would cause a donnybrook. An old tune sung by patrons leaving Quidi Vidi on Regatta Day had a chorus:

> Coming home from the races,
> Bleeding noses and cut faces,
> and we're all as drunk as blazes,
> Coming home from the Pond.

REGATTA NEARLY COLLAPSED

The St. John's Regatta ran into serious difficulties during the early 1930s and many thought the problems threatened its actual survival. In addition to the problems of raising finances each year to run the Regatta, the boat clubs had the ability to shut down the races if they chose to do so.

Prior to its incorporation in 1936, the Committee's influence over Regatta Day was restricted because of its limited control in raising finances and no control over the boats or boathouses. The Committee was elected on an adhoc basis each year and could only raise money by soliciting contributions from private individuals and businesses. The boat clubs owned the boats and the boathouses and had the exclusive right to operate cash wheels at the races to raise funds for their operations.

The boat clubs could shut down the Regatta by refusing to permit use of their boats on Regatta Day. It nearly came to that during the early 1930s. This lack of Committee control infuriated Committee members especially Rendell W. Jeans who was elected President of the Committee in 1935.

Up to then, the Committee had full responsibility for running the Regatta and accepting all financial risks, but were not able to assure that the Regatta would be held.

Jeans felt that the Committee needed to take over all the boathouses and boats in order to assure the survival of the Regatta. This would, however, cost a lot of money and the banks were reluctant to lend to a Committee that existed on an adhoc basis. The answer was incorporation. In 1936, with the help and support of Mayor Andy Carnell, incorporation took place and the future of the Regatta was strengthened.

At the time of incorporation, interest in the Regatta had fallen to its lowest level in decades. There was difficulty in getting full crews for the six-oared boats and sometimes races had to be cancelled. To deal with this problem, Jeans initiated the purchase of four new four-oared boats. The number of six-oared races was reduced and every second race was a four-oared race. The incorporated Committee was appointed by the Mayor and limited to fifty members. The boat clubs cooperated and in a short time the Committee took over the boathouses and boats. To do this they arranged a bank loan which was liquidated by continuing the yearly collection and operating cash wheels.

The four-oared races were not popular and were discontinued after several years. By that time, interest was revived in the Regatta. The Committee purchased a new six-oared shell, the *Coronet,* which was the last one constructed by the great builder, Bob Sexton. The Committee also made arrangements with the Star of the Sea Boat Club to take over the *Blue Peter*, which they owned at the time.

The Telegram, in an article printed prior to the Regatta of 1937, praised the work of the Committee in doing so much in such a short period of time and ending its first year with a credit balance and all accounts paid. It stated,

> The year 1936 must be looked upon as one of the
> most important since the institution of the Regatta in

St. John's. In the past, certain years produced events that made these years outstanding but when those of the future are recording the history of our annual Regatta they will have to set 1936 on a pedestal to itself.

That is true for many reasons. The year saw the Committee being elected on a new basis which gives it more of an air of authority; it saw for the first time the Regatta Committee become owners of boats and boathouses; it saw the construction of four new boats of a new type, and above all it saw the Committee make the initial steps for the improvement of the property surrounding the lake which culminated in a Committee being formed for the purpose of converting the property into a park which to future generations will be known as King George V Memorial Park.

In addition to purchasing new race boats and new judges' boats, the incorporated Committee built a new boathouse. They also built the Higgins Memorial Marquee on the north bank. The octagon shaped bandstand was built in 1937 by contractor A.G. Wornell.

The two club-owned boathouses near Boathouse Lane were purchased by the Committee and funds were raised to construct a new boathouse. The site for the new boathouse was made available through Gordon Winter, agent for the landowners. George Cummings was the architect for the building, which was constructed by contractor B. Stokes. The new boathouse was not just a shelter for the boats (as the old ones had been) but a central facility which included a work area, dressing rooms, a meeting room, and a canteen.

The official opening took place on Wednesday, July 26. Heavy rain and winds forced officials to move the event inside. Mayor Harry Mews performed the ribbon-cutting ceremony in the storage room as *Up the Pond* played in the background. Committee chairman Jim Higgins passed over the keys to the new building to Jack Ryan of the Boathouse and Pond Committee.

POLITICS

An interesting sidelight of Regatta history is that although Newfoundland became a province of Canada in 1949, the Canadian Army Band in St. John's was not invited to play at the 1949 Regatta. Music for that day was supplied by the US Army Band. And in 1948, Newfoundland's last year as a British Colony, the same honour went to the US Band who shared the day with the Mount Cashel Band.

FANS CAUSED TROUBLE

The ancient practice of allowing spectators on the pond in their own boats caused problems for the Regatta Committee in 1839. Supporters of an opposing crew interfered with the *John Crow* as it turned the buoy and caused the boat to lose the race. The crew complained and the stewards ordered a rematch. The *John Crow* lost to the *Henry*; a boat owned by Harbour pilot Captain Henry Gallishaw. A second incident occurred in the race between the *Maid of the Mist* and the *Red Rover*. The *Newfoundlander* reported, "On going down the lake, a boat not in the race ran into the *Red Rover*. We believe it to have been with malicious intent, and we should gladly see the parties instigating or committing acts like this to be brought before the public and punished." The stewards ordered a rematch and in a closely contested race, the *Maid of the Mist* won. Incidents like these led to the outlawing of spectators on the pond on Regatta Day.

LAND DISPUTE

At a time in the 1880s when the north bank was privately owned, one of the owners threatened to bar the public from using the land on Regatta Day. The owner of Woodley's Farm was upset because, just weeks before Regatta Day, fans attending a cricket match destroyed his unharvested hay and vegetables. Cricket fans regularly used the north bank path as a short cut to the cricket grounds at Pleasantville.

A member of the Regatta Committee pointed out that a strip of land fifteen feet wide on the margin of Quidi Vidi Lake was public property and noted that unfenced land is common, and there can be no trespass on a common. He pointed out that Woodley's land was unfenced on the lake side and asked, "Can there be any trespass on this land?" He warned that if Woodley went ahead with his threat he would be breaking the law by infringing on the fifteen feet of public access at lakeside.

Woodley settled his dispute quietly with the city. The dispute, however, inspired land owners to charge a rental fee for use of their land. Operators had to first obtain a permit from the magistrate in order to sell alcoholic beverages and a license fee had to be paid.

HOLY CROSS

Fans of the Holy Cross rowing crew were disappointed in 1961 when Holy Cross rowing in the *Royalist* crashed into the *Telegram* carrying the St. Pat's crew. The boat took on water and the west end boys had to row fast for shore.

A repair crew from the boathouse fixed the damaged *Royalist* and it was back in competition within an hour. However, many fans were disgruntled when the William Summers crew was assigned to the *Royalist* in the Championship Race. The Summers crew, known as the Monarchs of the Regatta, was the most popular crew of the era. Speculation was rampant that the damaged boat would hinder the crew from winning the championship. The determined and experienced Summers' rowers proved the speculation wrong by rowing their way to their third straight championship win.

THE CURSING CREW

The win by the Placentia crew in 1877 left one crew cursing mad. The Broad Cove (St. Phillip's today) crew went to Quidi Vidi fully confident to show themselves masters of the lake. When they lost the race to Placentia, they blamed the defeat on their boat the *Queen of Beauty*. They made no effort to conceal their feelings and their cursing and swearing could be heard by spectators in the vicinity.

The rivalry among crews on Regatta Day sparked many challenge races in the nineteenth century. In this case the Outer Cove crew, amused at the conduct displayed by the Broad Cove rowers, issued a public challenge to them. In a letter to the *Morning Chronicle*, dated August 13, 1877, and signed by William Lewis of Outer Cove, a challenge was issued.

It read:

> The Broad Cove men, not having been successful at
> the last Regatta, made use of strong language in order

to depreciate the value of the *Queen of Beauty* (in which they rowed). In consequence of it I would ask you to be good enough to insert this letter which I think will convince every impartial judge that the crew, and not the boat, was in fault, judging from the following facts: The *Queen of Beauty*, in the Fishermen's race, turned the buoy first, the *Placentia* and *Volunteer* next, and the *Native* three lengths behind them, which necessarily would give the *Queen of Beauty* a good start up the pond before the *Native* turned, (but the Broad Cove men say it) she lost her capability to row down by the buoy, and consequently those super excellent Broad Cove men came in fourth instead of first; but who would believe them when they say that the boat was good going down and bad coming up; no one but they would believe that those self-opinionated but flatulent Broad Cove men were not blessed with that energy and stability which are the required essentials for beating their opponents, and therefore winning the laurels of the day. In conclusion, if the Broad Cove men think they lost the race in consequence of the boat, let them accept the accompanying challenge, and then establish their right to superiority.

The Challenge: I, the undersigned, do hereby challenge, by putting the Outer Cove men in the *Queen of Beauty*, that they will row the Broad Cove men for fifteen pounds. The place and distance to be decided on between the two crews when other necessary arrangements are made.

William Lewis, August 13, 1877

The challenge was not accepted.

THE DISQUALIFIED CREW

An interesting story regarding a crew that illegally rowed in a Regatta of the 1930s has often been told during Regatta season and has become part of our colourful Regatta folklore.

The incident is said to have occurred in the intermediate race on Regatta Day. The crew involved had worked and trained long hard hours to prepare for the day of the races.

Minutes before the race, the unexpected happened. The crew had to make a sudden change in the boat, and without advising the Committee, took their position at the starting line.

The crews lined up and the starter raised the gun and prepared to fire. But he hesitated and looked around, then he lowered the gun without firing.

Spectators were curious as they watched the judges huddle in the Committee boat and the rumour rapidly spread that there was something illegal about the race. The uncertainty of the situation was dispelled when one of the judges shouted, "There's a chap in the boat who isn't registered. You're disqualified." The crew was ordered to return to the boathouse and the race was to proceed without them.

But the crew was not ready to let all their hard work go down the drain. Stunned by the decision, they remained at the starting line. The gun fired and the other crews were off in a flash. As they moved down the pond, and the band played *Gary Owens*, the illegal crew watched in despair.

However, caught up in the excitement of the moment they ignored the judges order and set out down the pond determined to get into the race. They were just as determined to win...by hook or crook.

The race suddenly turned into one of excitement. The illegal crew was rapidly catching up with the others. An East End crew took the lead at the buoys. The illegal crew were in last place, but quickly stepped up their pace. They caught up with and passed the third place boat, then the second place crew, and moved in on the first place rowers.

Near the bandstand, the two crews appeared to be neck and neck. The crowd on the banks had taken notice and the band playing *Up The Pond* stirred the excitement of the crowd. The illegal crew pulled ahead and were first over the finish line. They were greeted with lusty cheering from the throngs on shore. The East End crew and the judges looked on in disbelief.

The winners were disqualified but their spirits were not dampened. They left the pond happy that they had shown themselves to be the best on the pond. It mattered little what the judges thought and the loud cheering from the banks was enough recognition.

St. John's Regatta early 1900s. Photo courtesy of City of St. John's Archives.

CHAPTER FOUR

Regatta Mysteries

*I remember the old-time Regattas
and it's many a night that I spent
with the flickering light of a candle
to put up the frame of a tent.*

Old Time Regattas by Ed Cooper,
St. John's, 1921

THE 8:40 RECORD CLAIM!

With almost 200 years of history and tradition, it is inevitable that the Regatta would have a good share of mystery and controversy. The most common controversies surround the starting date of the Regatta, the course length, and the actual number of Regattas held. There is also the mystery of how Sir Edgar Bowring became recognized as donating the north bank of Quidi Vidi Lake to the city for one dollar while records show a direct transaction between Sir Edward Morris and the city for an amount much more than one dollar. Another mystery is how a Quidi Vidi Ladies crew became recognized as being the first ladies to row in a Regatta while history shows they never participated in an organized Regatta Day program. A little known claim that the pond was rowed in the remarkable time of eight minutes and forty seconds is also reviewed in this chapter along with the questions, "How did Quidi Vidi get its name? How many Regattas can we actually document as having taken place? And a WWII secret that reveals a near tragedy in St. John's on Regatta Day 1944.

By delving into a year by year examination of Regattas from the 1820s and reviewing old City Council records, I am able to shed new light on these mysteries.

WAS THE TIME OF 8:40 ROWED AT THE RACES?

In 1901, several days after the Outer Cove crew rowed the course in 9:13, a veteran of earlier races argued that the course had been rowed in the 1870s in the time of 8:40. The following article is taken from the *Daily News* of August 9, 1901. A correspondent writes as follows:

The daily papers today in connection with the Regatta, announced that the Outer Cove fishermen in the championship race rowed the Pond in the quickest time of 9:134/5, beating all previous records. While congratulating the crew and the Messrs. Job (owners of the *Blue Peter*) I write to tell you that the course was rowed in less time than that of yesterday. If my memory serves me right, I think it was the year 1872 that the outrigger shell boat *Terra Nova* was imported from Halifax by a couple of city gentlemen.

She was a clipper, indeed, and some of us older ones contend that her superior has never been seen on Quidi Vidi. The following year, 1873, she made time which has never been beaten. She was rowed by Mr. Ryan, at present City Council engineer, on the bow, Mr. E. Murphy, Mr. Roche, and Mr. Walsh now in the employ of Hon. J.D. Ryan. The other boats competing were the *Linnet* and the *Gasher*. They carried no coxswains, and the steering was done by the man on the bow. At the *Linnet*'s bow was Mr. Clapp, at one time a prominent figure in our Regattas.

He was a strapping fellow and when the gun fired he had such weight on his oar that he pulled the boat around, and Mr. Murphy's oar came across his back, so that in the first stroke it did not touch the water. The *Terra Nova*'s crew were too much for the others and soon left them astern. I cannot say if the course was the same length at that time as it is at present, but there seems to be very little difference.

The time in which the *Terra Nova* covered the distance that day was eight minutes and forty seconds. I believe that no official time was taken, but many who were at the Lake on that day will agree with me that the above is correct.

A memorizing feature in connection with this race was that when the winning posts were reached, Mr. Murphy in raising his oar, tipped over the boat, and the occupants were given a bath to cool their burning brows. I also think that one of the judges of this race was His Lordship Chief Justice Little.

A review of records of the era could not confirm this claim. During the 1870s there were many challenge races that were not part of the official Regatta and were not always covered by the press. Also, between 1871 and 1901, there were two *Terra Novas* that participated in the annual Regatta. The one that raced in the 1870s had a very poor race record and by no stretch of the imagination could be considered a superior race boat. The Committee denied the 8:40 claim. However, during the early part of this century there were many race fans who were convinced of its accuracy.

THE LADIES BREAK THROUGH

We'll meet at the Races
my old love and I;
and recall the dead dreams,
which bring many a sigh.
We'll talk of old times
and of when we were wooing
of how fate overtook us
and was our undoing.

Poem by Charles M. White, July 1922; Romance at the Races

Although the Regatta Committee has long claimed that the first ladies race to take place in the St. John's Regatta took place in 1856 it was actually 1949 that such an historic event took place. The claim that the ladies crew from Quidi Vidi Village participated in a Regatta Day ladies race in 1856 was based an old newspaper clipping combined with oral tradition over the past century that culminated in a formal induction of the crew into the Regatta Hall of Fame.

While there was a ladies race at the 1856 Regatta, it was not part of the official Regatta Day Program. The program that year scheduled ten races and a ladies race was not included. The ladies actually competed in a 'fun-race' after the official program had concluded.

The 1856 Regatta took place on August 13 and 14 (Wednesday and Thursday). Twelve races were held with seven being scheduled for the first day and five for the second. The additional two races, which included a ladies race, were spontaneous races thrown together and excluded from the official program. These type races were traditional during the first Regattas and were called Novelty Races or Bye-Races. It was a tradition dating from the first Regattas and its purpose was to provide amusement for spectators at lakeside.

That year the Regatta Committee met at Toussaint's Hotel de Paris on Water Street on July 29 to draw up its program, regulations, and to set a date for the Regatta. When the plans were finalized, they were published in local newspapers. The published official program con-sisted of ten races which included four- and six-oared races with participants from the following categories: Tradesmen, Amateurs, Set crews (Fishermen), and Amateurs under twenty. There was no mention nor sug-gestion in the program of any ladies race.

On Regatta Day the Committee published a notice that appeared only in the *Times* newspaper inviting those interested to participate in two Bye-Races. Registration had ended prior to this and all rowers having registered for the official program were required to pay a registra-tion fee. However, those entering Bye-Races were not required to pay any fees. The notice stated that provision had been made for two more races: a four-oared and a six-oared sealing punt scull race. Due to lack of interest the punt competitions were not held.

The regulations which were published along with the program a week before the Regatta itemized the conditions for competition in the official Regatta Day Program. The requirements included: a registration fee; registration dead-line noon on August 11; and at least three boats were needed for a race to be recognized. The regulations concluded that no boats would be registered after registration closed on August 11. The Quidi Vidi ladies did not meet any of the requirements which leaves no doubt that they were not part of the official program.

In addition to the above there were no newspaper references prior to the Regatta of any possible ladies race. The following newspapers were publishing in St. John's at that time: The *Times*, *Courier*, *Newfoundland Express*, *Newfoundlander*, *Public Ledger*, and *Royal Gazette*.

Prior to 1949, ladies had never participated in the St. John's Regatta Day Program. Since that time we have witnessed continual involvement and growth in the role the ladies play in this historic event. From no involvement to participation as rowers, coxswains, and Committee members represents the story of twentieth century women in Regatta history. One name which stands out as leading the way and inspiring female participation in the Regatta is that of Gert Reardigan.

Gert's contribution to Regatta history is reflected in her accomplishments over the years. She was instrumental in initiating the first ladies race in Regatta history. From there she continued to pioneer the involvement of women in the Regatta and during the process became:

The first lady coxswain in Regatta history.
The first lady member of the Coxswain's Association.
The first lady to cox a winning crew.
The first lady to cox a men's crew.
The first lady to cox a championship crew.
The first lady to cox a ladies championship crew.

The first lady to cox a midget championship crew.
The first lady to serve on the Regatta Hall of Fame Committee.
The first lady in North America to serve as coxswain in fixed seat rowing.

In addition, Gert Reardigan has the outstanding achievement of winning eleven awards in one year in fixed seat rowing (1978). Gert and Jack Reardigan are the first brother and sister couple to serve on the Regatta Committee. In her remark-able career serving the Regatta, Gert became the first lady role model in Regatta history. She is an extraordinary lady because of her dedication, hard work, and love for the Regatta. The Regatta was an important part of Reardigan family life. Her father rowed with the Catholic Cadet Corps; her brother Jack has served as rower, Committee member, and President of the Regatta Committee; and her nephew, Mike Summers, stands high among the great coxswains of Regatta history.

Gert Reardigan

POWDER PUFF BRIGADE

On July 7, 1949, according to the *Telegram*, spectators at Quidi Vidi rubbed their eyes in disbelief when they witnessed a four-oared race shell cruising over the surface of the Lake with a crew of women rowing. This was viewed as an extraordinary event.

The unusual scene was inspired by Gert Reardigan who suggested to her friends while at the old swimming pool at Quidi Vidi (east of present boathouse) that they seek permission to take a boat for a spin around the Lake. To their surprise permission was given and they found themselves in a four-oared shell with the noted coxswain Joe Smith at the 'till.' They delighted in the experience and several days later Gert was back with a crew of six looking for a six-oared race. This time the legendary coxswain Markie Marshall took the ladies for a spin on the Lake.

The girls were inspired by the practice and ran the idea of entering the Regatta to Mr. Marshall. He agreed and suggested that there could be a ladies race if enough women came forward to register. Gert and her friends spread the word and in a short time four crews had registered. The press, amused by the idea of women rowers, dubbed them "the Powder Puff Brigade." (The crews included Gert's East End crew, two crews from Quidi Vidi, and a crew from Bowring Brother's.)

Gert Reardigan, during her rowing career, competed at the Father Pippy Regatta in addition to the St. John's Regatta. The Father Pippy Regatta was traditionally held a week after the St. John's Regatta to raise funds for St. Joseph's Church.

The inclusion of ladies in the Regatta came at a crucial time for the St. John's Regatta. Interest was declining as evidenced by decreased registration for competition. There was not enough rowers for the Union, Press, and Club Races and the Committee was forced to make these joint races. Another indication of the low interest was the fact that there was no need for any elimination races in 1949. Ladies on the program sparked new interest.

Newspaper coverage of the 1949 Regatta Day activities described the race as one of the two highlights of that year's Regatta. The other being the championship win by the Higher Levels crew. The *Telegram* described the scene at the head of the pond at the conclusion of the ladies race, "Each contestant received a big hand for the splendid efforts displayed." Both the *Telegram* and the *Daily News* reported that approximately 8,000 fans gathered at the head of the pond for the ladies race. It was described as one of the largest crowds ever to assemble there.

Of the many tributes paid to Gert Reardigan during her career at the Regatta, the most impressive was that given by *Telegram* sportswriter Gord Follett who wrote, "She is one of the very few coxswains who would take any crew out for a spin if they were stuck. Quite often she ended up with the crews no other coxswain would take. But she put as much pride and effort into those crews as she did in her stronger crews.

"Gert Reardigan," he concluded, "is considered to be one of the most popular and considerate coxswains the St. John's Regatta has seen in 157 years" (*Evening Telegram* August 1978). Gert Reardigan is a worthy inductee into the St. John's Regatta Hall of Fame.

CHANGING BOAT STYLES

For decades it was a popularly held belief that racing shells were introduced to the Regatta in 1897 by Bob Sexton. While Sexton introduced a superior and faster race boat than those used in nineteenth century Regattas, it was actually a boat builder in the 1830s and 1840s who introduced the first race shells. That man was Samuel Loveys.

> But the famous Samuel Loveys now to you I will declare, He launched the handsome Ripple to compete in that same year. (1840)

Along with the *Red Rover*, *Lallah Rookh* so swift and strong,
With the Gem that came from Halifax to race the *Lucy Long*. (Jimmy Murphy 1910)

Sam Loveys

The name Samuel Loveys emerges from the nineteenth century Regatta history among the most influential and effective builders of the Royal St. John's Regatta. Loveys contribution to the evolution and endurance of the Regatta was as a boat builder. His innovation and genius in this area changed the course of Regatta history and reignited spectator interest at a period when it was on a decline. The story of Sam Loveys is the story of the transition of the type of boats used in our Regatta from those used in the daily commercial life of the colony to a style of boat specifically designed and built for racing.

From the first Regattas at Quidi Vidi in the early 1820s until 1842, the type of craft used in competition was solely the type of boats used in the everyday commercial and mercantile life of the colony of Newfoundland, and included pleasure crafts described as sailing yachts. These contests were very competitive and only cash prizes were awarded. However, a tradition of heavy betting quickly emerged and large sums of money exchanged hands depending on the outcome. The contests were generally viewed according to the *Times* newspaper of August, 1843 as, "...contests of superiority of the models of the boats, and the ability and skillfulness of the rowers." Emphasis, however, was on the superiority of the boats.

Regatta promoters sought out the fastest and best built boats to compete in the Regattas. During the 1830s, they had turned to Halifax boat builders in hopes of getting a boat that could dominate the day of the races at Quidi Vidi. The Halifax boats manned by local rowers were generally successful and in time the locals viewed their presence as a challenge to the national pride of Newfoundland.

The *Public Ledger* newspaper, August 22, 1839, speculated that interest that year increased due to the introduction of, "...a couple of crack boats from Halifax which were to dispute the palm with the native builds." The two boats, *Victoria* and *Maid of the Mist,* outclassed the native boats. The following year with the advent of the Regatta, the *Public Ledger* noted that the lack of competition in 1839 might result in a dwindling interest in the forthcoming Regatta. Referring to the previous year's Regatta it observed, "The mere racing of the boats did not create a great deal of interest as there was evidently too great a disparity among them."

Sam Loveys had already built several boats for earlier Regattas and this year hoped to make the Regatta more competitive by constructing a new boat which he called the *Ripple*. Loveys was held in high regard and his new boat stirred local enthusiasm.

According to the *Times* of 1840, it was the success of the Halifax boats which, "...inspired the great builder Sam Loveys to build the *Ripple*." The *Ripple* was built in the style of the traditional whaleboats of the era. Loveys had a reputation as a boat builder which he gained from building boats for commercial use. Records suggest that Loveys had built earlier boats for the Regatta but the records did not name them.

The *Times* of August 1840 reflected the notoriety of Loveys when it described the *Ripple* as, "A boat that reflects certainly much credit upon our native builder Sam Loveys who we feel confident has now fully realized his expectations respecting the speed of his boats." To meet the challenge set by Loveys, a new boat was imported from Halifax. The import was named *Lalla Rookh*, after a popular passenger boat operating across the Atlantic at the time. The builder changed the traditional whaleboat design.

The *Public Ledger* of the same month suggested that the Halifax boat was a little different in appearance than the traditional whaleboats used in Regatta competitions. The newspaper described it as, "...a peculiar build boat which gave her an advantage in still waters." In the Regatta of 1841, the *Ripple* held its own against the *Lalla Rookh* (*Public Ledger*, August 1841). While the *Ripple* proved to be a fast racer and credit to her builder, the *Lalla Rookh* quickly dominated the Regatta. In 1843 she won first prize in every race in which she competed. Loveys' *Ripple* won second place in every race competed.

The outcome of the races became so predictable that public interest began to decline and fans were frustrated. So bitter was the resentment to the Halifax built boats that just prior to the Regatta that year someone cut up the tent that housed the *Victoria*, hammered a hole in its bow, and stole its oars. Local fans looked to boat builders like Sam Loveys, Mike Kearney, and a Mr. Ould to build a superior boat that would regain "Newfoundland's National Pride."

Such was the background which influenced local builders in 1844 to make drastic changes in the design and construction of their boats. Loveys and Kearney individually set out to construct a boat specifically designed for racing. Although there appears to have been an effort to keep the designs secret, it wasn't long before the public became aware of the projects.

The *Newfoundlander* of August 1844 referred to Kearney's new boat, the *Ferryland Lass* as, "...an experimental gig built on a novel principle." The same paper described Lovey's boat, the *Lucy Long* as, "...a sanspareil," adding that, "the care and pains he has bestowed on her construction make him deserving of success." A third local boat entered that year was the *Quiz*; a traditionally designed whaleboat built by Mr. Ould.

The entrance of three new local boats combined with the change in design revived public interest in the Regatta of 1844. The outcome changed the style of boats used in the Regatta forever. Newfoundlander's lining the banks of Quidi Vidi for the races that year enthusiastically hoped to have their pride restored. They were not disappointed. By the conclusion of the two day Regatta, Loveys' *Lucy Long* emerged as the fastest boat ever seen on the pond.

Following a successful first day, the second day brought even more glory to Loveys' new race boat. The Regatta stewards decided to put a special race on the program to test the speed of the best boats of the Regatta. Five of the fastest boats of the racing fleet were chosen for the race. The outcome was as follows: 1st— *Lucy Long*; 2nd— *Lalla Rookh*; 3rd— the *Gem* (Halifax built); 4th— *Ferryland Lass*; and 5th— *Repeal* (Halifax built).

The next day the same boats competed again in the Sweepstakes Race. In this race the fastest boats were compelled to participate or else pay a fine to the Committee. The thirty-six foot long *Lucy Long* outperformed all others once again. Loveys' race-boat emerged as the model which local and Halifax boat builders emulated thereafter. The *Times* observed, "... the *Lucy Long* built by Mr. Loveys of this town, has proved herself to be by far the best boat on the Lake. Too much praise cannot be given to Mr. Loveys for the taste he has displayed in building her."

The *Public Ledger* also praised Loveys' work. It reported that Halifax had sent the crack boats here to compete with the native built boats and pointed out that Loveys proved, "...that we are not to be outdone in boat building by the architects of our sister colony." The following year newspapers again lavished praise upon Sam Lovey's. It was reported after the two day Regatta, "The *Lucy Long* we understand took the lead again yesterday. She certainly walks the water like a thing of life, and well may the native builder be proud of the symmetry of her proportions. This boat which we may now set down as A-1 may lead to a credible spirit of emulation and is likely to test the skill and ingenuity of persons in a neighbouring colony." (Nova Scotia) (*Times*, August 8, 1845).

Ten years later, improving his design, Loveys built another winner, the *Undeen*, which according to the *Public Ledger*, August 1854, "...was the top boat in all the principle races." Loveys followed this success in 1855 with another boat which he called the *Darling*. Following that year's Regatta the *Public Ledger* wrote, "...the *Undeen* and *Darling* built by Sam Loveys are the best on the Pond. We cannot forbear to state that these two beautiful boats were built in this town by Mr. Samuel Loveys and they certainly do place him in an advantageous position with regard to the 'crack boats' which have been imported. (The *Fly* had been sent from Halifax expressly to compete against the *Darling*.) That same year Loveys built two new pilot boats which competed in the Pilot Boat Races.

On July 27, 1855, the *Public Ledger* commended Loveys on his fine work. It stated, "This is creditable to him, and we hope will, as we think it certainly should, establish his reputation as a first class boat builder and consideration be tended to him accordingly." The innovative racers introduced by Loveys amused some people who resented the change in race boat styles. The *Public Ledger*, July 26, 1855, described the Regatta boats practicing on the Harbour, "The Harbour for some evenings past has been dotted with these variously painted fairy like things." When race-shells were introduced in 1844 they competed in the category of whaleboats. All references up to 1896 referred to these race boats as whaleboats as a matter of tradition. The Regatta Committee changed this practice in 1897. The *Telegram*, July 27, 1897, quoted a statement from the Committee, "The word 'whaleboats' will not be used in the programme, race boats will be substituted."

Sam Loveys initiated the change to race shells and influenced builders of the nineteenth century up until 1897 when Rendell and Sexton produced the *Glance*, a great improvement over Loveys design and started a new era of faster race-shells at the St. John's Regatta.

Loveys constructed his boats in his workshop at the head of Playhouse Hill (Queen's Road). Among those identified to date as Loveys built boats are the *Ripple*, *Lucy Long*, *Undeen*, *Darling*, and *Eugenie*.

THE UNBROKEN 9:13

The famous record of 9:13.8 set by the Outer Cove crew in 1901 has never been broken. The reason it has never been broken is that the course rowed at that time is not the same length as the course rowed today. The remarkable times set in 1981 and after which inspired a renewal of interest in the Regatta should actually be considered as new course records.

Throughout most of the last century, arguments over the course length were always settled by reliance upon the verbal history expressed by old-timers who were adamant that the course length had not changed since 1901. There were many who disagreed.

Only three official surveys of the Pond were known to exist and Regatta Committee records of the course length prior to 1919 were lost or destroyed. In 1951, an official survey was carried out by the City's Engineering Department which measured the course at 8,050 feet. Add 200 feet for turning and the official course length was 8,250 feet. However, lanes from stake to buoy were from lane one to four respectively 4,028 feet; 4,022 feet; 4,019 feet; and 4,017 feet.

In response to arguments over the course length, in 1990 Don Johnson, Captain of the Course, arranged for Hawco, King, and Byrne Surveying Company to measure the course and to set all lanes at the same length. The end result was a course that differed ten feet from the 1951 course. The Johnson-initiated survey measured the course from stake to buoy; 4,020.39 feet for a total of 8,040.78 feet. Add 200 feet for turning and the full course was 8,240.78 feet.

Prior to the Regatta of 1965, a prominent sports figure and sports historian Gordon Duff came across a survey of the Quidi Vidi Race course completed in 1924. He brought this and some other supporting information to the *Telegram* Sports Editor, Bob Babcock, and the result was a front page story with the headline, "Was the 9:13.8 possible?" Babcock, who was already convinced the course had changed over the years, concluded that the 1901 course was about thirty-five yards shorter than the modern day course. He based this on the differences shown when comparing the two surveys from 1924 and 1951.

Still, nobody really could say with any certainty the length of the pre-WWI race course at Quidi Vidi Lake. Over recent years after reviewing the opinions and available documentation on the course length, I reviewed the charts stored at City Hall and the 1924 survey had mysteriously disappeared. Without the 1924 survey, there appeared to be no concrete evidence to argue that the course had changed. At least that was the case until I came across an official proclamation by the Regatta Committee published in the *Telegram* on July 31, 1909. The Committee rarely made such public declarations and likely did so because there had been some questioning of the course length prior to and including that year.

The Committee declaration stated: The Honourable J. Harvey, President of the Regatta Committee, gave out full information last night as regards the length of the course as follows:

The distance from stakes to buoys........4,100 feet
Allowed for turning ....200 feet
From buoys to stakes............................4,100 feet

Total 8,400 feet or, one and a half miles plus
480 feet.

The 1924 City survey measured the existing markers
on the Pond that year and in doing so had determined
the course was not consistent with the pre-1914 course.
That survey, which showed the length from stake to buoy
as 3,900 feet, was incorrectly adjusted to 4,020.39 and
remained consistent until all race lanes were adjusted in
1990.

The Regatta, which started in the early nineteenth century, was interrupted from 1861 to 1870. In 1881, the
Halifax Recorder published an article on the St. John's
Regatta and described the course length as one and a half
miles plus 100 yards. The *Evening Telegram* reported the
same course length in 1881. Add 200 feet for turning and
the course of 1881 was 8,420 feet. That course length var-
ied only twenty feet from 1871 to 1914 when war broke out.

Prior to WWI, it was the job of a Committee member
to mark off the race course each year. He used traditional geographic locations to measure the race course. Since
there were no Regattas in 1915, 1916, 1917, 1918 and
1919, an error was made in setting the course-length five
years later that has never been officially recognized or
corrected.

The race course of 1901 was 160 feet longer than the
course rowed over in 1981. Historically, the 1901 Outer
Cove 9:13.8 record stands as the record for the old race
course which was altered in 1919. It is a recognized fact
in sports that records can only be made or broken where
the course remains consistent. The Regatta Committee
itself recognized this principle in 1973 when it refused to
recognize the Hefferman's Ladies crew's time of 5:12 as
a record. That time tied the existing 5:12 held by the
Hotel Newfoundland Ladies in 1958. Yet, despite
protests from the Hefferman's crew, the time was never

recognized as tying an existing record. The reason given was that the course for the Ladies Race had changed. Not only was the principle recognized here but the Hefferman crew were not inducted into the Hall of Fame for the same reason.

The opportunity to break the 9:13 ran out in 1914 and consequently it remains the record for the old course length and can never be broken over the current race course. An interesting sidenote to Regatta history is that the Outer Cove crew of 1901 rowed in only one Regatta. The 1901 Regatta was the first time they rowed as a crew and the following year only three of them returned to compete. They were John Whelan, J. Nugent, and D. Croke. They never rowed together as a crew after 1901.

(Heffernan's 1973 crew were Paul Ring, cox; Mary Oakley, stroke; Rosalind Power; Mercedes Connors; Joan Buckle; Yvonne Oates; and Florence Haire. The Hotel Newfoundland 1958 crew were Albert Joy, cox; Bernice Lacey, stroke; Vera Smith; Jean Wilson; Patsy (Connolly) Leonard; Jean Dawe; and Elsie Worthman.)

St. John's Regatta 1880. Photo courtesy of the City of St. John's Archives.

OLD COURSE RECORD

T he *Eugene* built by Sam Loveys in 1856 recorded the time of 9:41 in the late 1850s. This record remained unbeaten until Outer Cove rowed the 9:20 in the *Myrtle* in 1885. However, the *Morning Chronicle* of August 11, 1877, gave credit to the time rowed that year by Placentia as being the Regatta six-oared record. The newspaper article noted, "The shortest time of the day, 10 m 28 sec., was made by the Placentia crew, which is also the shortest on record for whaleboats." (All six-oared racers were under the category of whaleboats until the late 1890s.) Some Regatta writers over the years refer to this as the record which Outer Cove broke in 1885 with their time of 9:20. However, in 1881 a Fishermen's crew rowing the *Dora* recorded the time of 9:49.

The time amazed the public and newspaper reports in Newfoundland and Nova Scotia noted the event as an accomplishment. The following excerpt from my book *Up The Pond* (Creative Publishers, 1992) describes the reaction,

> 'When the six-oared whaleboat *Dora* rowed the mile-and-a-half plus 100 yard course at Quidi Vidi in a time of 9:49, it was reported in both the Newfoundland and Nova Scotia press. People seemed amazed that these boats could travel so fast. They measured forty feet long and three feet six inches wide with varying depths of thirteen to sixteen inches.'
>
> (Evening Telegram, August 19, 1881)

In 1883 Outer Cove rowing in the *Volunteer*, built by Philip Mahoney, set a new record time by rowing the course in 9:46. In 1885 it was Outer Cove again which set a new record and again in a Phil Mahoney built boat named the *Myrtle* in the time of 9:20.

UNKNOWN RACE REVEALED

For more than 100 years it has been part of Regatta history that there were no races from 1861 to 1870. However, while reviewing newspapers of that era I discovered that a boating competition was held on St. John's Harbour in 1865. The race featured a four-oared competition with the Milroy Four rowing against the Hayward Four. The race resulted from a public challenge made by Sam Milroy and accepted by Jim Hayward. The event attracted much attention and townsfolk went out on the Harbour in boats to witness the race. In keeping with boat-race tradition, there was spirited betting on the event. Hayward's crew rowing in the *Firefly* defeated the Milroy Four. Sam Milroy was involved in reviving the Regatta at Quidi Vidi in 1871.

NEAR DISASTER OF 1944

The thousands of people who lined the banks of Quidi Vidi had no idea how close the City of St. John's had come to a major disaster that day. On Thursday, August 3, 1944, just minutes after the gun on Signal Hill fired to announce to the people of St. John's that the Regatta was going ahead, gun fire erupted in St. John's Harbour.

The Harbour was filled with local boats and naval boats from several nations. Suddenly, gun fire erupted from somewhere on the Harbour and a crew of workmen on Southside Road scrambled for shelter. The bullets went whizzing by and some struck the oil tanks on Southside Hills. The incident could have caused a catastrophe had they penetrated the tanks. The source of the gun-fire and potential disaster remained a secret until after the war.

Declassified records described the incident in St. John's Harbour on Regatta Day, 1944. The gunfire originated on board the HMS *Dianthus,* a Canadian Corvette moored near the southside of St. John's Harbour. The vessel was scheduled to move out to sea that morning where a drill was to take place to train crewmen on the handling of guns. Despite concern expressed by crewmen, the captain ordered them to load the Pom-Poms (ships guns). In addition to fuel tanks on the Southside, there were many military vessels in port. Some of the crew was worried over the possibility of an accident occurring during the loading process.

Just after the flag went up at Cabot Tower and the Signal Hill gun sounded to announce 'a-go' for the Regatta, rapid gun-fire was heard from the Harbour area. While loading Pom-Poms, the gun accidentally went off and several of the bullets struck the oil tanks. Realizing the danger, a crewman from St. John's lowered the gun so it pointed away from the tanks and then shut it down. Before the gun-fire stopped, however, it sprayed bullets over the heads of civilians on shore.

Fortunately, there were no injuries. The *Dianthus* went to sea and completed its practice on schedule. Meanwhile, another successful Regatta was recorded and those attending had no idea of the near tragedy at the Harbour. Most of the naval ships in port that day carried large quantities of ammunition.

THE EARTHQUAKE

Did an earthquake strike St. John's during the Regatta at Quidi Vidi in August 1898? The following is an article published in the *Evening Telegram* during August of that year:

Did anyone notice a trembling, as if an earthquake, at seven o'clock on the morning of the Regatta? At that hour the signalman on the Block House, Mr. Michael Cantwell, having just hoisted the colours announcing the steamer *Iceland* was arriving, when he certainly felt the whole structure vibrate and a noise as if a sudden gust of wind had struck and shook the place.

He walked out of the apartment and looked up at the flag. It was hanging idly up and down the mast, and scarcely a breath stirred the atmosphere. Wondering what the matter could have been he re-entered the room, and was no sooner there than the phenomenon occurred a second time.

He finds it difficult to explain the strange occurrence except upon the hypothesis of it being two shocks of an earthquake. So far, as is known, nothing of the kind was experienced in the town. The motions continued for about two seconds each, and there were about twenty seconds between each occurrence. A week later a resident of Victoria Street told of similar activity in that area which caused his house to tremble.

THE SHOWER OF QUARTZ

Just days before the Regatta of 1872, rowers were prevented from rowing on the pond by a severe hail and snow storm. It occurred on the Friday before Regatta Day which that year was held on July 30. The storm had an astonishing aspect to it. According to a letter published in the *Newfoundland Chronicle* on August 2, 1872:

A large number of small pieces of quartz fell in the vicinity of the River Head Convent (Convent Square) and on the Marine Promenade (Water Street West at Railway Station). Actual, veritable quartz, differing

in size, the largest I have seen being nearly half an
ounce in weight.

By Regatta Day good weather had returned and it
was ideal for a successful event. The hail storm and
quartz phenomena were the main topics of conversation
around lakeside that day.

THE FIRST REGATTAS

We have known for more than fifty years that the earliest record of a Regatta at Quidi Vidi is found in the
Mercantile Journal of 1826, and for at least thirty years it
has been known that a rowing match took place on St.
John's Harbour in 1818 (also found in *Mercantile
Journal*). While it has been a popular belief in the city
that the races at Quidi Vidi were a continuation of those
held in St. John's Harbour, Regatta historians have not
yet been able to verify that connection. In view of this, I
find it a real stretch of the imagination to accept that the
Quidi Vidi Regatta is a continuation of the 1818
Harbour rowing match. Although the St. John's Regatta
Committee in 2002 recognized a single-race held on the
Harbour in 1818 as the starting date of the St. John's
Regatta, this standard is not one recognized elsewhere.

There is mention in the *Mercantile Journal* in 1816 of
a rowing match on the Harbour that year. During July
2002, I found an item in the *Royal Gazette* of 1810 referring to a sailing match on St. John's Harbour that year.
(This is the earliest record found of a boating competition in St. John's.) The starting point for that race was
Hutton's Wharf and contesting boats were distinguished
by a red pendant at the main.

Sailing competitions were also part of the first Quidi
Vidi Regattas. Those first Regattas were two day events

with rowing on the first day at Quidi Vidi and sailing races on the second day at St. John's Harbour. It may be argued that the 1818 event inspired the founding of a Regatta at Quidi Vidi. But it is also possible that the Quidi Vidi Regatta pre-dates the 1818 Harbour rowing match. It seems the early Harbour races involved people accustomed to hard labour and rowing who in that era were considered the professionals of rowing. The Quidi Vidi Regatta was founded by the amateurs of rowing (those not involved in hard labour who included clerks, merchants, and professional people). Indeed, the advertisement in the *Mercantile Journal* of 1826 called for a meeting of the amateurs of rowing to organize that year's Regatta. This tends to support the theory that the Quidi Vidi Regatta was founded by a group other than those who organized the 1818 Harbour Race.

Although the records of the starting date of the Quidi Vidi Regatta have disappeared, there were many attempts during the first part of the twentieth century to fix a starting date. Historian H.M. Mosdell claimed in 1922 that Regattas were held on Quidi Vidi Lake as early as 1828. In 1931 the public was informed by C.J. Ellis, Committee President, that the Regatta started in 1851. He based this on records in the possession of the Regatta Committee that dated back to 1851. In 1946 a *Telegram* reporter unearthed proof that a Regatta was held in 1826. In his article he cited the *Mercantile Journal*, August 4, 1826, contained the earliest known record of an actual organized Regatta being held at Quidi Vidi. Although this was a significant discovery, it was ignored by officials for years. The year 1828 had somehow become accepted as being the earliest Quidi Vidi Regatta.

Official recognition that Regattas were held earlier than 1828 came after a prominent sports figure and sports historian. Jack V. Rabbitts published a full page article on the Regatta in the *Telegram* on July 18, 1964.

In the article he mentioned that he had made a significant find while researching Regatta history. He was referring to the *Mercantile Journal*'s 1826 coverage of that year's Regatta. The author did not give any credit to the 1946 *Telegram* discovery.

The Regatta Committee soon recognized 1826 as the date of the first Quidi Vidi Regatta based on the 1826 *Mercantile Journal* account. *The Royal Gazette*, the first newspaper in Newfoundland was started in 1807 and the *Mercantile Journal* began in 1816. Between 1807 and 1826 the only mentions of boat racing events on St. John's Harbour were in 1810, 1816, and 1818. However, there are many missing issues between 1807 and 1826. There are references to coverage of the Regatta in a third newspaper, the *Sentinel*, but no copies of that newspaper have survived. Yet, the neglect of mentioning a Regatta may have been related to publishing policies at that time. The *Mercantile Journal* started covering the Quidi Vidi Regatta in 1826 after organizers paid for advertisements in that paper. Although nobody can yet pinpoint the actual starting date of the Regatta, I feel it can be shown that it was already a tradition at Quidi Vidi by 1826.

While researching nineteenth century records, I discovered some interesting information to support claims that the Regatta at Quidi Vidi was being held earlier than 1826. The combination of five newspaper accounts from 1826 to 1829 support this claim. The *Mercantile Journal* of August 1826, upon which the Regatta Committee had over the years based its recognition of 1826 as the starting date, refers to the Regatta even in that year as being an annual event. It stated, "The St. John's Annual Regatta commenced on Monday with rowing matches on Quidi Vidi Pond pursuant to public advertising."

The *Public Ledger* of August 17, 1827, also suggests the Regatta was already established. It reported, "We do not observe any active preparations for the Races, which are usually held at this season of the year. As a friend to occasional popular amusements we cannot suggest that at the present moment, more than under ordinary circumstances, the observance of this 'annual recreation' is particularly desirable. We throw out the hint for the consideration of those who have been accustomed to taking a leading part in these engagements." Soon after a Regatta was held.

The *Public Ledger* of August 1828 suggests Regattas were held before 1826. That paper reported on the boycott of the Regatta that year by the ladies of St. John's. The article stated, "The women of the town boycotted this Regatta, and not because of the weather. We feel assured it was just a retaliation upon their parts for the inattention with which they have been treated for the last three or four years."

The *Royal Gazette* of August 1829 describing the 1829 Regatta noted that the gentlemen of the town, "...as usual made it a point to dine together on that occasion." This point also suggests a Regatta which even in 1829 had been a tradition. Another referral to a continuing Regatta is found in the *Public Ledger* of August 21, 1829. The editor stated, "We would suggest to our readers that the time is arrived when some arrangements should be made for the usual observance of our annual popular amusement." The 1829 Regatta was held on Thursday, September 10.

Records to date cannot pinpoint the exact starting date of the Regatta. However, there is ample evidence to show that boat races were held in St. John's Harbour as early as 1810 and at Quidi Vidi earlier than the recognized 1826 date. In that era, Quidi Vidi was outside St. John's and some townspeople complained the Regatta was too far from the town. As late as 1947 most of the pond was still outside St. John's. The city's border stretched from the smokestack at the old General Hospital to the large cross at Mount Carmel Cemetery.

In regards to our Regatta's place in rowing history: even considering the starting date of 1826, the Royal St. John's Regatta is the oldest fixed seat rowing Regatta in the world. It is also one of the oldest surviving Regattas in the world.

Compare the St. John's Regatta, which we know was a tradition in 1826 with starting dates for other world famous Regattas:

The Royal Hobart Regattas	1827
The Oxford-Cambridge Regatta	1829
The Henley Regatta	1839
First US Regatta	1845

All of the above were interrupted at one time or another due to war or national calamities.

Two boat-racing competitions older than the Quidi Vidi Regatta are the Oxford-Eight (1815) and the Doggett Coat and Badge in 1715. However neither are recognized as Regattas by Oxford University. The United Kingdom classes private fixtures as races, even if several are run and regattas tend to be open or largely open in terms of who can enter. The Doggett event is a single-scull type match. The Oxford-Eight is not an open competition.

HOW MANY REGATTAS HELD?

While the Royal St. John's Regatta Committee recently recognized 1818 as the starting date of the Regatta, neither Committee nor historians over the decades have been able to tell the exact number of Regattas held since that date.

Prior to 1871 the Regatta was held intermittently and official records did not survive over the years. Some were lost in the several fires that destroyed the city and others just disappeared.

Several years ago Don Johnson asked me if my research into nineteenth century Regattas was able to determine the exact number of Regattas held. I reviewed the boxes of notes I had gathered over the years but to answer Don's question with any confidence I found it necessary to review nineteenth century records again. It was already common knowledge that there were no Regattas held in 1940; during World War I; the 1892 fire; and the 1860s, but among that those who attempted to answer the question could offer only rough guesses.

One aspect of researching old Regattas which quickly became obvious was that in the absence of preservation of official records, the primary material for research of nineteenth century races was the newspapers of the day. While Regatta records had disappeared, most newspapers from 1807 onwards have been preserved. For each Regatta held from 1826, newspapers reported the popular sporting-social event in editions published the day after Regatta Day.

A secondary source of research material was the published memories of old-timers which appeared years, sometimes decades, after the event. These proved to be helpful but inaccurate in details. One such article in 1901 had a retired rower living in California claiming that he had witnessed a race on the pond in 1871 in which a crew covered the course in eight minutes forty seconds. If such a record was ever made, it was not done so during an officially held Regatta. Other old-timers mentioned anecdotes having taking place in years when there had been no Regatta.

Relying solely on newspaper records of each Regatta published a day or two after the event, I have determined that from 1826 to 2002 we have had 148 Regattas. Historian H.M. Mosdell, M.B., recorded that for the first fifty years the Regatta was held intermittently. He was correct. Newspapers reviewed included the *Royal Gazette*, the *Mercantile Journal*, the *Courier*, the *Times*, the *Patriot*, the *Newfoundlander*, the *Public Ledger*, the *Chronicle*, the *Daily News* and the *Evening Telegram*.

There were no records to support that Regattas had been held in the following years:1830, 1832, 1833, 1834, 1835, 1836, 1837, 1846, 1847, 1848, 1849, 1850, 1861, 1862, 1863, 1864, 1865 (there was a rowing match at St. John's Harbour in 1865), 1866, 1867, 1868, 1869, 1870, 1892, 1915, 1916, 1917, 1918, and 1940. A total of twenty-eight years with no Regattas.

If calculating the number of Regattas from 1826 subtract twenty-eight. If calculating from 1818 subtract thirty-five. (We have no record of Regattas in 1819, 1820, 1821, 1822, 1823, 1824, and 1825.)

THE WEDNESDAY TRADITION

The first Wednesday of August has been considered the traditional day for holding the St. John's Regatta and occasional suggestions to change it have been met with quick public condemnation. However, this was not the traditional day for our Regatta during the nineteenth century. In fact, the first Regattas were not held on a set day or month. Early records show that the date for the Regatta was influenced by the annual hay harvest. It seemed that almost everyone had an interest in harvesting hay to feed their horses and farm animals. Each year a public notice appeared in the newspapers inviting interested parties to a public meeting. At this meeting a Committee was elected to plan and raise funds to hold the Quidi Vidi Regatta. All prizes on Regatta Day were cash prizes.

Horses were the means of transportation and were also necessary for the everyday trade of the city. Usually the harvest took place in August and the beautiful mead-ows in and around the city were beehives of activity. Regatta organizers chose to await the completion of the hay harvest to hold the day of the races.

Although the Regatta pre-dates 1826, that year marks the earliest known records of a Regatta at Quidi Vidi and by 1839, the hay harvest continued to influence the choice for Regatta Day. The *Newfoundlander* on July 25, 1839, reported on the formation of the Regatta Committee that week for the 1839 event. It noted, " The date for the Regatta was not set. But no time will be lost after the hay harvest which, promising to be so much earlier this year than usual, will probably enable the Committee to name some day not later than August 20." The 1839 Regatta was a two-day event held Wednesday and Thursday, August 21 and 22. The harvest was over and the weather was beautiful.

The first Regattas were two day events often held on Monday and Tuesday with rowing matches held at Quidi Vidi Lake on the first day, and sailing competitions held at St. John's Harbour the second day. During the nine-teenth century Regattas were held on varying dates between July 23 and as late as September 10. The date for the Regatta continued to vary during the 1840s but the days changed to Thursdays and Fridays and usually around mid-August. The hay harvest remained an influ-encing factor up until 1840.

In 1852, organizers experimented with a three day Regatta. This was met with strong opposition from busi-nessmen and the Total Abstinence Society. In 1856 the two-day Regatta was held on August 13 and 14 (Wednesday and Thursday). Due to political unrest in the colony and the violence this had caused in St. John's, there were no Quidi Vidi Regattas from 1861 to 1870. Boat racing, however, did take place on St. John's Harbour in 1865.

When the Regatta resumed in 1871, it was a two day event held on the first Thursday in August followed on Sunday by a Regatta on the Harbour. The Quidi Vidi portion of the Regatta during the 1870s and 1880s was held mostly on Thursday's, and usually before mid-August. One was held during the last week of July.

While the 1890s saw most Regattas being held on Wednesdays, the first week in August had still not become a practice. The 1890 Regatta was held on July 23. During this decade one Regatta was held on Tuesday and another on Thursday. During the first twenty-five years of the twentieth century, the tradition of Wednesday took root. There was, however, more experimentation before it was accepted as the set day for the annual Regatta.

In 1926 the Regatta was rescheduled to the first Thursday in August. During the 1920s, the port of St. John's was busy with passenger ships going to and from the US and Canadian ports. Unfortunately, the arrivals in St. John's were on Thursdays, too late for the Regatta. In 1926 the Committee set the first Thursday of August as Regatta Day. Several ships carrying almost 2,000 visitors, mostly former Newfoundlanders, arrived in port that Thursday.

This was changed, however, in 1929 to the first Wednesday of August because of the problems it caused for businessmen. Because Regatta Day was a civic holiday, employers found it hard to get enough men to unload the ships in port. The Committee faced more problems when high winds caused a two day delay and it finally was held on Friday, August 9. On Wednesday the Committee was unable to inform the public in time and as a result many people turned up at the Lake and missed work.

The Regatta was almost abandoned in 1930 because of a dispute among the private boat clubs. In addition, there was dwindling public support for the Regatta. This was attributed to the motor car, gambling, and train excursions. Because of the confusion surrounding the on-and-off again Regatta of 1929, stores decided to remain open in 1930 until a go-ahead was confirmed. A half-holiday was given. Wednesday was the choice of the business community because they were required to give workers a holiday and Wednesday was the slowest day of the week. The first Wednesday of August became entrenched in the 1930s and has remained a tradition since then.

THE BOWRING CONNECTION

One of the mysteries of Regatta history has been how Sir Edgar Bowring got recognized for donating the north banks of Quidi Vidi Lake to the people of St. John's, when records show that the land was owned by Sir Edward Morris and deeded by him to the City of St. John's. Sir Edgar's role in saving the North Banks was even enhanced to the point where claims have been made that he actually donated the land to the city for the sum of one dollar.

The story of the North Bank being saved, thereby ensuring the continuation of the Regatta, goes back to 1908. At that time the North Bank was privately owned by about fifteen individuals who allowed it to be used by the public each Regatta Day. However, in 1908 when reports reached Prime Minister Edward Morris that plans were being considered to turn the land into a private development, he took immediate action to prevent that from happening.

Morris raised the $11,129 purchase price of the land by mortgaging his Beaconsfield Estate with the Bank of Montreal to obtain the money at five percent interest. In addition some prominent friends of Morris guaranteed the loan. Morris did not want the land for himself. He expected that some wealthy citizen would be willing to take it over and develop it as a park for the people of St. John's.

By 1914, Morris was having problems paying the interest and it was at this time Sir Edgar Bowring stepped forward and paid off the bank in full. He promised to convert the area into a park for the public. Bowring was known for his benevolence and ranked among the most respected men in all Newfoundland. Part of his plan included moving a boathouse owned by Total Abstinence Society which divided the property. He made a generous offer to the Society, providing them with a new boathouse at the head of the Lake. The Society accepted the offer. However, an unexpected event abruptly ended Bowring's plans; World War I.

Ten years later, the war had been over for six years and it appeared that Bowring's plans had been forgotten. Some members of City Council were concerned that the property would again fall into the hands of private developers. This concern prompted the City Council to appoint a Committee to look into the possibility of purchasing the land from Bowring. The results of that meeting are recorded in the minutes of Council's private meeting on October 30, 1924.

Sir Edgar no longer had any intentions of turning his land into a park, purchasing a new boathouse for the Total Abstinence Society nor donating the property to the people of St. John's. He responded to Council's interest by offering to sell the land to the City for $11,129 the exact amount he initially paid for it. Council minutes state, "...he (Bowring) thought that in the interest of future generations this land should be reserved for citizens and that the city would not be in any way hampered as regards to purchasing it, as rentals for grazing etc. which would be received would pay the interest on the outlay." As a result, Council began negotiations to purchase the property.

With negotiations in progress, the Newfoundland Government on November 27, 1924, agreed to advance to the City of St. John's the $11,129 needed to purchase the North Bank of Quidi Vidi and add the amount to the consolidated debt at the, "...usual interest rate." When Sir Edgar was advised that the City now had the money to complete the deal, the negotiations took a curious twist.

Sir Edgar was unable to provide the deed to the property. He had never actually acquired ownership of the land even though he had paid for it. At the private Council meeting of December 18, 1924, Sir Edgar advised Council that the papers were in Lord Morris' possession, "...and that it would take little time to obtain it." He then made a peculiar request of Council. Sir Edgar asked the City to pay him for the land before the end of the year (1924) even though he had not produced the deed. He did however offer to, "...indemnify the Council against any loss which may arise from non-production of the necessary documents." Bowring's integrity was unquestionable and Council had no problem accepting the offer.

However, at the private Council meeting on December 31, 1924, the mood changed. The City had acquired the funds from the Newfoundland Government to buy the land but Sir Edgar was still unable to produce the deeds. Councillor J. Martin argued that Council should have all the necessary papers in order before finalizing the purchase. To the chagrin of Bowring's lawyers, they had learned that although Sir Edgar had assumed the debt on the property with the intentions of acquiring it to turn into a park for the people of St. John's, the ownership was never transferred to him. Sir Edward Morris still held legal title to the land. A motion to withhold payment to Bowring until deeds transferring ownership from Sir

Edward Morris to Sir Edgar Bowring were submitted, was defeated. Council did, however, adopt the condition that the cheque would only be issued when Bowring submitted the plan of the property to Council. Bowring complied and the money was paid. Council accepted Sir Edgar's indemnity and requested the deeds and transfers be acquired and submitted to the City as soon as possible.

On March 19, 1925, C.J. Ellis Honourable Secretary of the Regatta Committee, obtained Council's permission to proceed with the preparatory work of improving the Lakeside at Quidi Vidi at the Committee's expense. Meanwhile, on March 12, 1925, Bowering's solicitors Messrs. Warren and Winter submitted the draft of the deeds for the Quidi Vidi property and expressed the expectation that, "...the matter would be finalized as quickly as possible."

The matter had become an embarrassment to Council, Sir Edgar Bowring, and Sir Edward Morris. Bowring had innocently negotiated the sale of property he did not own. City Council had paid him knowing he did not have the deed and Sir Edward Morris continued to hold the deed to it.

To deal with the quandary, Sir Edward Morris signed over the property directly to the City but did not collect any payment. The payment that had been issued to Sir Edgar stood as payment for the land. Lord Morris transferred ownership on March 31, 1925. However, the conveyance was held and not actually registered until June 23, 1938. The legal mess surrounding the transfer was hidden in the records of Council's secret meetings. In 1998 I sought and received permission to research the records of these secret Council meetings. Based on my findings, this mystery of Regatta history is now solved.

LAST WILL AND TESTAMENT

Several years ago Sir Edgar Bowring was inducted into the Royal St. John's Regatta Hall of Fame. The suggestion that he had sold the property to the City for the sum of one dollar remains part of his nomination. Bowring was generous to the people of St. John's and is best remembered for the gift of Bowring Park to the City. He passed away June 23, 1944, at the age of eighty-four. He left an estate in England valued at £418,695 sterling. The duty paid on the estate was £164,518 sterling. His charitable bequests included £2,000 sterling to Bowring Park for improvements; £2,000 sterling to the Church of England Orphanage; £1,000 sterling each to the Roman Catholic Orphanages and Methodist Orphanages; and £500 to the Salvation Army; all of St. John's.

THE NAME KITTY VITTY

Oh, just down behind the city,
In a vale, so bright and pretty
Lies the lovely Kitty Vitty
Basking in the summer day.
O'er thy bosom, swift and flitty,
Sped by arm, and muscle gritty,
Song, and joke, and laughter witty,
Bounds the pleasure boat away.

(Archbishop M.F. Howley)

No book on the history of the St. John's Regatta would be complete without some discussion on the name Quidi Vidi and its origin. Dr. E.R. Seary in his scholarly work on place names of the Avalon Peninsula examined the many variations of the name as recorded in old documents and concluded that the most likely source was a French family name with several variations Quidville, Quedville, Quiedville, and Quetteville.

The late A.B. Perlin, respected historian and newspaper editor, disputed Seary's claim in his Wayfarer's Column (August 1966). He argued, "I doubt that any Frenchman or Jersey man was identified with the settlements in and around St. John's in the seventeenth century. Dr. Seary identified many variants of the name. They include: Quilliwiddi (1671), Kitte Vitte (1675), and Quide Vide (1677).

The *English Pilot* published in 1689 referred to two variations of the name; Quidi Vidy or Kitty Vitty. H.W. LeMessurier, who researched and collected Newfoundland history during the early part of the twentieth century, came to a different conclusion as to the origins of the name. He argued that the name might be a corruption of Guy's Divide, or a line separating John Guy's Plantation from that which had been subsequently formed in St. John's. Another respected historian of the nineteenth century, Rev. Dr. Moses Harvey suggested a widow named Kitty Vitty had operated a public house in the village and the place got its name from her. Little credibility is attached to Harvey's explanation. Archbishop Howley, who carried out extensive research into Newfoundland nomenclature, suggested the most likely name had been Qui Dividie which he translated as 'here divide.'

Howley's claim was considered credible by Perlin who observed, "I have always felt that Quidi Vidi got its name because it was the first opening in the wall of rock immediately north of St. John's. I am not a linguist and I don't know what the Portuguese word would be for the place that divides but it may have been something like Qui or Qua Divida. And almost all the early variations tend to suggest something of the sort. It follows that, as in the case of so many other place names in Newfoundland which have been distorted by the untutored English, Qui Divida or Qua Divida could have become either Kwidi Vida/Kiddy Viddy and from Kiddy Viddy it is but a short move to Kitty Vitty."

The earliest reference to the name can be found in the journal of James Yonge, who served as surgeon to the fishing fleet in the 1660s. Yonge, who first visited Newfoundland at the age of fifteen, kept a journal of his stay. In 1669 while operating out of St. John's he wrote, "...during our being here I went once to Petty Harbour and twice to Kitty Vitty of which place I forebear a description, intending to leave that to the figures (maps) by and by, to be made of all the harbours I have been in this land."

Originally, Quidi Vidi was a plantation owned by John Downing. A census of 1682 spelled the name as Quitevide. In 1679, a statement written on behalf of the people of St. John's relating to its defence spelled the name as Que de Vide. It stated that, "...to fortify St. John's, naturally very strong, with twenty-five guns and 200 small arms and some small arms to defend the creek Que de Vide to prevent surprises."

In the French report on D'ibberville's capture of St. John's the name was spelled Kerividi. Dr. Seary refers to the usage of Kitty Velle by Captain Cook in 1763. However, in Cook's chart of 1775 it is spelled Quidy Videy. No doubt the debate over the correct pronunciation and the origins of the name Quidi Vidi will continue which in itself is another colourful aspect of the historical Regatta at Quidi Vidi.

CHAPTER FIVE

The Merry Regatta

Do you want to hear the band,
playing the Banks of Newfoundland?
It will put smiles on your faces;
Are you going to the Races?
Do you want to view the scene,
of all the tents upon the green,
where you will meet familiar faces;
Are you going to the Races?

Tom Delahunty, 1952

LIKE CHRISTMAS

The Regatta is celebrated with the same enthusiasm and anticipation as the Christmas Season. Music, dancing, and food were part of the event and its popularity attracted a host of intriguing visitors. The people of St. John's looked enthusiastically towards the first Regattas at Quidi Vidi in the 1820s and 1830s. Some would go to the Lake days ahead and set up tents. On the north side of the Lake there were Coaker's and Bulley's farms with acres of barley, oats, potatoes, other vegetables, and berries. Popular musical instruments of the time included fiddles, tin whistles, and drums. Every tent had its own music. On Regatta Day the charm of the area was increased by the sight of hundreds of camp fires near the Lake to cook family dinners. This custom lasted into the 1940s.

At the end of the day many went to Coaker's Farm for a picnic and dance. The Royal Artillery Band entertained throughout the day. There was no bandstand for the group and they had to play on dry ground at the foot of the bank near the Governor's Marquee (near where the bandstand is today). There were some concession tents but always an ample supply of liquor.

Today, Newfoundlander's all over the world identify the *Banks of Newfoundland* or *Up The Pond*, as it is more commonly called, with the Regatta. However, over the first several decades of the Regatta, fans tapped their feet to a different Regatta Day theme song. It was the Irish ditty, *Rory O'Mour*. Today the Irish tune *Gary Owens* is played at the sound of the starting gun signalling to the crowds on the banks that a race has started, while the *Banks of Newfoundland* is played as the crews pass the bandstand on their return to the finish line. The music *Gary Owens* was also General Custer's marching tune.

FANS ON THE LAKE

During the first Regattas, spectators were allowed on the Lake in their own boats during the races. They rowed alongside the participants and frequently interfered with rowers by taking their oars, ramming the boats, or passing a spare oar to a crew which had broken one.

Two main tents, which were the largest on the grounds, dominated the scene at the early Regattas. One was for the Stewards and the Committee that ran the event. The other for the Governor and his friends. The *Newfoundlander*, July 24, 1855, described the scene at the 1855 Regatta: "The North and West bank of the Lake gave evidence of the interest felt in the sport by the inhabitants; and upon the brow of an ascent on the North was seen conspicuous above all, the Standard of Old England waving over a Marquee expressly for His Excellency the Governor who with his family and suite, honoured the sport with his presence."

THE FARMS

Nearing the end of the nineteenth century the north side was privately owned by farmers who opened their doors to the public on Regatta Day. The north side, spanning an area from Mount Carmel to Pleasantville, was occupied by three large farms owned by J.L. Ross, Bill Woodley, and R. Routledge. On Regatta Day they welcomed the public and served hot food at a dollar a plate. People could enjoy meals of turkey, geese, fowl, roast, lamb, fresh vegetables, tea, coffee, and aerated water. The farms had dancing galleries and, to the tune of *Turkey in the Straw* played by fiddlers accompanied by tin whistle players, patrons danced throughout the afternoon and sometimes into the early hours of the following day.

Those who ran out of their own supply of liquor could buy both imported and home brews at Lakeside. Others would gather at the Bunch of Grapes Inn on the site now occupied by Regency Towers. According to the *Times*, August 9, 1877, "The whole town population could be seen pouring down toward Quidi Vidi in a continuous stream of carriage, cars, and shanderdans of all makes and sizes."

With the revival of the Regatta in 1871, the Committee was concerned over the reputation of old Regattas for their rowdyism and alcohol abuse. Their response was to introduce Temperance Drinks. While malt beers with a strong alcohol content were popular, the Temperance Groups pushed non-alcoholic hop ale and winter stout.

MUSIC AND DANCING

During the 1870s the idea for a Grand Regatta Ball originated and lasted into the 1950s. After British troops left Newfoundland in 1871, Professor David Bennett's Band took over the tradition of supplying Regatta Day music. In 1877, the Regatta Grand Ball was held at the Victoria Rink with Professor Bennett's Band in attendance. The next day Bennett's Band was given help at Lakeside by a visiting British Naval Band.

The brass band of Professor David Bennett was the first non-military big band to play at the Regatta and they dominated the Regatta scene throughout the 1870s, 1880s, and 1890s. When Bennett retired, Professor Power took over. Power had played with Bennett's Band for more than a decade before leading his own band during the first years of the twentieth century.

Power was succeeded by Art Bulley and the Catholic Cadet Corps Band and the Mount Cashel Band. Sometimes local bands shared their duties with visiting military bands. Several British and German Bands played for Regatta Day and gave their version of *Up The Pond*.

There were many brass bands in St. John's during the early nineteenth century and they often competed for the honour of playing at the Regatta. In 1912, among the bands applying for the right to provide Regatta Day music were the City Band, the Total Abstinence Band, and a couple of individual-led brass bands. The Committee awarded the honour to the Total Abstinence Band.

In the 1940s, with the arrival of the American Forces, American Military Bands became part of the annual Regatta Day. Canadian Military Bands played for at least one of the Regattas of the 1940s and a series of pre-Regatta band concerts. In the 1950s the American and Mount Cashel bands provided music at the Regatta. The Newfoundland Regiment also played in the 1960s and the CLB took over in the mid-1960s and have been a fixture at the Regatta since.

The Grand Regatta Dance was traditional and continued into the 1950s. It was the main Regatta night celebration but there were many other celebrations throughout the city on Regatta night. No recorded music in those days. Twenty-five to thirty-five piece brass bands gave an elegant air to the occasions. Sometimes, two big bands played at the same place on the same night. The Grand Regatta Dances were held at the Gaiety, Prince of Wales Arena, Star Hall, Catholic Cadet Corps Hall, the Prince's Rink, and the St. John's Memorial Stadium.

During the 1920s and 1930s emphasis was on old time dance music and the latest tunes from New York. Some of the musical numbers of the era included: *My Castle In Spain; Is a Shack In the Lane; Carolina Moon; My Angeline;* and *Chiquita.* The various rowing crews tried to outdo each other in decorating the dance halls to create a festive appearance.

The popularity of the Regatta had spread far and wide and in 1927 movie clips were made by the Pathe Movie Company of New York and Hollywood and shown in theatres throughout North America. In the 1930s, a ferry boat took people across the Harbour to the Narrows Tea Rooms at Fort Amherst to eat, dance, and be serenaded by the Maestros or the Steven's Swing Band. The first Grand Regatta Dances held at the newly built Memorial Stadium in the early 1950s featured the Kenny Brothers and their Princess Orchestra, one of the most popular bands of the time. Jessie Earle, Newfoundland's answer to Dinah Shore, was a popular singing performer at Regatta Dances and popular as well were local musical greats like Myra Frelich, Mickey and Freddy Michaels, Mickey Duggan, and Joe Murphy (also known as Barry Hope).

VISITORS

Throughout a history that spans three centuries, many interesting and intriguing people have turned up at Lakeside on Regatta Day. Perhaps the most intriguing of these was a Jesuit Priest who earned world-wide recognition as a scientist.

Father Perry, who visited the 1874 Regatta, was leader of an international expedition of astronomers to the South Seas between 1874 and 1882 to observe the transit of Venus. Perry was in control of two man-of-war ships throughout the expedition. His work enabled science to fix the exact distance of the sun from the earth within a few miles. At Lakeside, he told a reporter he was, "...enraptured with the beauty of Quidi Vidi Lake."

In 1906, Earl Grey, the Governor General of Canada, visited the Regatta. He was escorted around the lake in a Victoria Carriage. To honour the visit, spectators wore rosettes of silk with a miniature photo of the Earl. The

Governor of Bermuda, Newfoundland-born Sir Ambrose Shea, visited the 1890 Regatta. Shea had rowed on the Lake in the Regattas of the 1850s.

John Keefe, who was born in St. John's and who had become rich and prominent in the city of Chicago attended the 1886 Regatta. Before moving to the United States in 1880, Keeefe worked as a cooper in St. John's. He became a multi-millionaire through real estate investments. Keefe owned, among other properties the Park Manor Housing Development at Hyde Park, Chicago.

A celebrity at the 1946 Regatta was a prominent and well-known American author-broadcaster named Mabel Cobb. Cobb had written a series of popular children's books and also hosted a popular radio program in Boston and New York. Cobb was born in Grand Falls.

Perhaps the most famous visitor to the Regatta was Cyrus Field; the man credited with being the force behind laying the first Trans-Atlantic cable. Mr. Field attended a Regatta in the late 1850s, possibly in 1857 following the failure of his first attempt to lay the cable.

FROM WASHINGTON

Bill Lawlor was a native of St. John's working in Washington in 1947. On the eve of the Regatta, Lawlor was overwhelmed with the desire to be at lakeside the next day. He contacted some high-ranking friends in the military who got him on a military plane leaving Washington that day at 4:30 p.m. and by 10:30 a.m. Regatta Day he was rubbing shoulders with friends at the Regatta.

Sir Cooper Key was a distinguished visitor to the Regatta of 1876. Sir Cooper commanded several British Naval Ships in port that year. He was delighted when his crew from the HMS *Bellerophan* won the Naval Race. Sir Cooper truly enjoyed the Regatta with all its novelty attractions and sporting competitions. He returned the following year and his crew won the Naval Race for the second year in a row. The British troops were especially welcomed in St. John's in 1877 for a big favour they performed for St. John's. During his visit in 1876, authorities discussed with Sir Cooper Key the obstruction to the Harbour caused by Merlin's Rock. Sir Cooper promised at the 1876 Regatta that he would be back to remove the obstruction thereby improving the entrance to the Harbour. Merlin's Rock was located at the narrows of St. John's Harbour and large ships experienced great difficulty entering and leaving the Harbour because of it. In 1877 Sir Cooper kept his word and using dynamite blasted Merlin's Rock to a depth of thirty-feet.

DYNAMITE DUNN

Tom 'Dynamite' Dunn, was a great Regatta enthusiast. He had gotten the nickname 'Dynamite' from his wrestling days when he became a world famous sports figure. The popular comic strip Joe Palooka was inspired by the career of Dynamite Dunn. Dunn had a big following in the US which prompted cartoonist Mel Stevens to base a syndicated comic strip on the Newfoundland wrestler. The original strip had Dunn's fight manager as Joe Jenks and Tom Dunn as Dynamite. After Stevens passed away, Hans Fisher took over the comic strip and changed the name Joe Jenks to Knobby Walsh, Dynamite to Joe Palooka, and made Palooka a boxer instead of a wrestler. Many of the comic strips were based on true happenings in Dunn's career.

THE BOSTON VISITOR

Johnny Bray was on the banks of Quidi Vidi when a crew from Placentia defeated local rowers in 1877. He moved to Boston a year later and did not visit Newfoundland nor attend another Regatta until fifty years later in 1927. By then he had become a sporting legend in the Boston area. At the age of sixty, he won the swimming championship of New England. In doing so, he defeated thirty-nine competitors and was the only one to complete the twelve mile marathon swim in adverse weather conditions. Although hundreds tried to duplicate Bray's achievement up to 1927, it had remained unbeaten. He was treated to a hero's reception by, Mayor Curley, who awarded him a silver cup and medals in a ceremony at the Keith Theatre in Boston.

LOST AN OAR

A thrilling race took placein 1951 in the American Service Race which caused many to compare it to the CLB Broken Oar Race of 1901. The Supply Squadron, while rowing up the pond, lost an oar near the swimming pool near the present day boathouse. Cox Frank Breen wouldn't allow his crew to give up and he inspired them to complete the race which they did by coming in first. They won by four boat lengths. Other crews in that race included the Torbay Outcasts, the Stokers, and a crew known as the AACs.

THE AMERICANS

For almost twenty years, Americans at Fort Pepperrell on the banks of Quidi Vidi Lake played an active and supportive role in the annual St. John's Regatta. Although long departed from our shores, the era of the American Forces is worthy of recording. The story of how Newfoundland became a site for American bases during World War II is an interesting and important part of British and Newfoundland history.

The USAF Base in Newfoundland was conceived when by executive agreement on September 3, 1940, the US traded fifty four-stack flush deck destroyers, veterans of World War I, in exchange for ninety-nine year leases of British Bases in the West Indies, on Antigua, Jamaica, the Bahamas, British Guiana, and Trinidad; in addition the US received as gifts the right to bases on Newfoundland and Bermuda. A note from Lord Lothian, British Ambassador to the United States, to Cordell Hull, US Secretary of State, on September 2, 1940, making the offer and Mr. Hull's note of the same day accepting had paved the way for the agreement.

It did not take long to issue orders which would implement the trade. Colonel Maurice D. Welty, Infantry, was appointed as the Commander of the garrison in October 1940. Units from the 3rd Infantry Regiment, 62nd CA (AA), and the 57th CA together with special troops were to form the original garrison at Pleasantville.

Early in January 1941, the actual work of organizing the garrison for transportation to St. John's was begun. January 15, 1941, was a very busy day. The headquarters and headquarter detachment of the Newfoundland Base Command was activated and the Financial Section was organized on board the US Army Transport *Edmund B. Alexander*, the ship designated to bring the garrison to St. John's. The medical detachment was organized and 'A' deck of the *Alexander* was designated as the hospital and detachment barracks. The *Alexander* left the New York port and moved to Bayonne, New Jersey, for further loading.

On January 19, 1941 at 12:30 p.m. the *Alexander* left Bayonne and anchored in New York Harbour at 2:45 p.m. On this same day the full staff of the Newfoundland Base Command was announced with Colonel Maurice D. Welty, Commanding Officer. The first chaplain of the base was First Lt. Francis E. Hand.

The *Alexander* sailed out of New York Harbour at 6 p.m. on January 20, 1941, bound for St. John's, Newfoundland, carrying the first American troops going overseas to occupy new bases. In a howling blizzard the transport-ship arrived off St. John's Harbour on January 25, 1941. The weather and the narrow entrance to the Harbour combined with the size of the *Alexander* prevented the ship from making harbour for four days. On January 26, 1941, the Officer's Club was established while on board the *Alexander*.

She docked on January 29 and Colonel Welty went ashore to make official calls. Temporary headquarters remained on board the *Alexander* and by February 15, construction was underway at Pepperrell and twelve sheds had been completed. Two others were built on the south side of Quidi Vidi Road. By April 3, water from Windsor Lake was being furnished to the US settlement at Quidi Vidi. The *Alexander* was opened for public inspection on April 7 and approximately 4,000 persons were shown around the ship.

While waiting for construction of facilities at Pepperrell, the Americans made arrangements to move to Camp Alexander. Camp Alexander, named for the Mexican War Commander of the 3rd Infantry, was leased from Carpasian Park Limited. and consisted of fifteen acres of land. The lease was signed on April 15, 1941.

The base at Quidi Vidi was designated Fort Pepperrell on April 23, 1941, in honour of Sir William Pepperrell, an American colonial soldier. On May 20, 1941 the Headquarters, Newfoundland Base Command, was moved to 44 Rennies Mill Road from the *Alexander*. At the same time units started to move from the *Alexander* to Camp Alexander. The Finance Section moved to a barn at Camp Alexander. The movement of troops from Camp Alexander to Pepperrell began on November 24, 1941, and during December 1941 the Officer's club was opened there.

In March 1943, the Americans were granted land along Quidi Vidi for the duration by the St. John's City Council in return for post war assistance in beautifying the site. The outstanding event of 1943 was the establishment of Radio Station VOUS, White Hills. The White Hills property had been purchased for $120,365. By January 1944, VOUS was in operation and many local citizens along with its American staff members participated in its broadcasts.

In 1945, the Americans constructed a fence along the north side of Quidi Vidi Boulevard and turned the Lake front property back to its owners. During the early years of the Americans stay on the banks of Quidi Vidi, they provided a separate sewage system for the Quidi Vidi settlement which ran directly into the ocean.

Shortly after arriving in 1941, while awaiting construction of Fort Pepperrell, the Americans operated their Military Police Headquarters from offices above the old York Theatre on Water Street. In 1942, the base was visited by British Dominion Secretary and later Prime Minister of England, Clement Atlee. The same year the popular Mayor of New York City, Fiorello La Guardia, visited the base as chairman of the Joint Defence Board of the US and Canada.

The St. John's Golden Arrow Bus Company put new busses in operation between the City and Pepperrell on October 7, 1942. For almost twenty years the Americans participated in the racing competitions at the Regatta. Their splendid musicians provided music from the bandstand for most of that period. They often shared this duty with the Mount Cashel Band.

Lt. Col. Timothy J. Regan, on July 2, 1945, addressing American Forces at Pepperrell made the following commentary:

> When the base was first constructed it looked as though the enemy would overrun Britain. They already had weather stations in Iceland and Greenland. Their submarines were running practically unchecked in the North Atlantic. The actual and immediate danger to Canada and the US was very real indeed. A base from which we could protect our eastern cities and factories was number one priority in our defence plans. The answer to that was Newfoundland. This has become a clenched fist challenging the Germans to come any further. The Germans were driven from Iceland and their stations destroyed on Greenland after the Newfoundland Base was secure. While you were here and seeming to be inactive, your very presence was helping to keep the European War confined to Europe.

CHAPTER SIX

Boats and Builders

First Race-Shells, cheer after cheer,
they rent the air from lusty throats so
proudly.
The hills around caught up the sound
in echoes long and loudly.
Then we did draw the pure champagne
a sparkling glass overflowing
while all did note 'Speed to the boat!'
Then off she went a-rowing.

Jimmy Murphy, 1906

FIRST BOATS

The boats used over the first decade of Regatta history had no resemblance to the shells of today. They were the standard types used in the commercial life of the colony and included whaleboats, jolly boats, punts, gigs, and sail-boats.

By the 1840s, organizers were making efforts to improve the Regatta and they sought the development of special race boats for use at the Quidi Vidi event. Competition was keen between St. John's and Halifax to build the best and fastest boats for the Regatta.

During the 1840s and 1850s the following boats were built at Halifax and shipped to St. John's: the *Victoria*, *Lallah-Rookh*, *Banshee*, *Gem*, *Repeal*, and *Fly*. The boats were not identical in size and weight. The *Lallah-Rookh* was a six oared, thirty-five foot long shell.

NINETEENTH CENTURY
BOATS AND BUILDERS

The top boat builder of ancient Regatta's up to the appearance of Bob Sexton on the scene was Sam Loveys. He built the shells during the 1840s and 1850s that competed with the Halifax-built shells. Loveys built the *Ripple*, *Lucy Long*, *Undeen*, *Darling*, and *Eugenie*. It was Loveys *Undeen* that stopped the reign of the Nova Scotia built *Banshee* during the early 1850s.

Other less well known local boat builders included the Holdens (father and son team), Lewis, Johnson, Bethune, Vinnicombe, O'Rourke, Phil Mohoney, John Ryan, F. Mallard, and Father Pat O'Brien.

These early racing shells met with some opposition when first introduced at the Quidi Vidi Regatta. The following editorial appeared in the St. John's newspaper *The Patriot* just before the 1854 Quidi Vidi Regatta.

> We like the amusement, particularly when coupled with something practical to be gained. But we cannot see what good can be attained by the exhibition of racing qualities of boats such as those generally run on the lake.
>
> For any practical purposes in the business of the colony they are perfectly useless...they are good for nothing except displaying a good deal of ingenuity in the manufacture. If we are to have aquatic sports in the shape of boat racing, let the boats be those used in the stable trade of the colony — a race between good whaleboats or punts used in the fishery, rowed by the hands who usually row them, or a race between our swift sailing fishing Jacks or Western Boats would be practical and exciting and tend to the promotion of good fishing boat building.
>
> But a race between construction of pasteboard, however ingeniously put together and rowed by quill — drivers can never tend to any benefit and is at best an idle and useless diversion.

The suggestion was not heeded and the shell type racers were improved upon and developed and became the only boats used in the Quidi Vidi Regatta.

When the Regatta was revived in 1871, after a ten year hiatus, there was no shortage of good race boats and boat-builders for the Regatta. During the 1870s, there was Fred Lewis who built *Lady of the Lake* and Ned Sinnott who built *Placentia* (renamed *Contest*). *Hawk* was owned by John Ryan and *Mary Glover* by the Dryer family. In the 1880s a series of new boats was added. These included *Dora*, 1881, the *Native* built by Mr. Bethune in 1883, and the *Volunteer* built by Phil Mahoney 1883. In 1884 Mahoney built his best racer and called it *Terra Nova* (renamed *Myrtle* after the 1884 tragedy referred to earlier in this book). The City Club purchased *Avalon* in 1886 and the team of Herder and Halleran built *Gypsy* in 1888. Another Regatta boat builder was Richard Holden who built the *Indian Chief* which he made for an Indian girl.

In 1882, *Olivette* went on the pond and *Lady McCallum* built by F. Mallard of Quidi Vidi Village was added to the fleet of racers that same year. Philip Mahoney was back in 1890 with a new boat christened *The Iris*. In 1894 Mahoney took great pride in launching his newest boat *The Daisy* (forty-one feet long) and put it on display at Newman's Wharf at St. John's Harbour. The *Daisy* was similar in design to *Dora* and *Myrtle*. By 1897 the City Club owned *Cabot, Iris,* and *Glance*. The Southside crew purchased *Cabot* from the City Club for ten dollars.

PHIL MAHONEY

In time Phil Mahoney emerged as the best boat builder of that era. Mahoney, who sometimes had the help of one of his brothers, built many race-shells used in the Regattas between 1871 and 1897. The two, who lived on Southside Road, built their boats in a large cooperage owned by the father of Canon Bolt on Patrick Street just up from St. Patrick's Church. Phil Mahoney was the Bob Sexton of his day. He sometimes purchased the oars for his boats at the auctions held at the Market House (site of present day Court House). For his boat, the *Jenny Lind,* he purchased a sixteen foot long set at the auction. Father Pat O'Brien of Bay Bulls, who had a reputation in the Maritimes as a yacht designer in 1901, built the *Shanawdithit* in a work shed on Convent Square off Hamilton Avenue. The design was wider than the Sexton boats and lacked their speed. Father O'Brien was an expert naval architect who had designed a clipper that won races against some of the best in Canada and the United States. His clipper served as a model for boats that made history on the Grand Banks. He wanted to design a clipper to beat the famous *Bluenose* but could not raise the money to complete the project.

BOAT SIZES

The following is a sampling of the boat measurements from the 1870s to 1890: the *Iris*, 1890, forty-one feet long. In 1881, the *Dora* was forty feet long, three feet six inches wide, thirteen to sixteen inches deep, and was 800 pounds in weight. In 1877 *Placentia*, renamed *Contest*, measured thirty-four feet long, three feet ten inches wide, and seventeen inches deep. *Lucy Long* was thirty-six feet in length.

Halifax-built boats played an important role in the first fifty years of Regatta history. The top Halifax boat builder for the St. John's Regatta was a man named Moseley who built the *Gem*, a top racer of the era. Other boats of that period both Halifax and local included *Lallah-Rookh, Lucy Long, Banshee, Quiz, Ripple, Repeal, Ferryland Lass, Undeen, Darling, Indian Girl*, and *Jenny Lind*.

IT'S THE BOATS, NOT THE ROWERS

Throughout most of the nineteenth century it was the boats rather than the rowers that were considered the primary factor in winning at the Regatta. This is a fact recognized in the following excerpt from *The Evening Telegram*, July 1884:

The belief is a general one that tomorrow rowing will be a test of the men rather than of the boats. The latter are now pretty well all of the same class of build, and dimensions, and this is especially true of *Volunteer, Terra Nova,* and *Resolute* in whose beams and depth there is scarcely a variation of an inch or so, and whose 'go' is similar.

This is a great gain on the condition which determined victory in all our former Regattas, in which the best boat, manned it might be by an inferior crew, had the advantage, not of their own skill and strength but the advantage of their boat beating their superiors with the oar. Now however, the crews in the three boats named meet on even terms and the struggle between them must be regarded, not so much a test of the boat, but a test of the men.

The other four competitors: *Buttercup, Olivette, Forget-Me-Not,* and *Fishermen* are wider in the beam and their chances greater in smoother than in rough waters.

The *Halifax Recorder* of August 9, 1881, reported on the type of boats and rowers of that period. The article stated:

At St. John's, NF, Wednesday, there was a Regatta on Lake Quidi Vidi, the principal event of which was a race in boats called whaleboats, which were forty feet long, three feet six inches wide, and varying in depth from thirteen to sixteen inches; the average weight is 800 pounds.

The great race of the day was pulled by the rival fishermen of the different outports. It had its origin in 1860, when the Prince of Wales paid his first visit to the land of Cabot, and established a Prince of Wales prize to be annually competed for by the fishermen of Newfoundland.

The whole course covering one mile and a half plus 100 yards, involving, too, a complete turn mid-way, was rowed over in nine minutes forty-five seconds, in boats of extraordinary weight and without outriggers, sliding seats, or any of the other aids with which aquatic science has supplanted the strength and skill of the oarsmen.

THE LONGBOATS

In 1895 the Bob Sexton-built boat, the *Glance,* first went on the Pond. Its presence at the Quidi Vidi Regatta stirred public controversy which had not been witnessed since 1844 when Sam Loveys broke with tradition and introduced the first race shells. The *Glance* was designed by Dr. H.H. Rendell, who designed many of the Sexton boats. Measuring forty-nine feet in length, the *Glance* was longer and sleeker than any boat that had ever raced in a St. John's Regatta up to that date.

The Committee viewed the new boat with skepticism and most felt the style was not at all suitable for the Regatta on Quidi Vidi Lake. One member with experience in boat building commented, "Her low freeboard fore and aft will no doubt cause her to swamp unless there's a smooth pond." Another added that the boat was too long to be able to turn the buoys. He explained, "She's too low in the water and she'll swamp before she gets to the buoys. Maybe she'll do well in smooth water with a straight no-turn course like the English row."

Rendell brushed aside the criticism and replied, "Gentlemen you are about to see the quickest turn ever made at the buoy and I sincerely hope that on that day the water will be rough. Then you will see the safest boat on the pond come through with flying colours." The pre-Sexton-built boats required a quick short stroke to keep them moving and they dipped their bows and raised their sterns considerably when the oars were being driven through the water.

The sarcastic and critical mood of Committee members and many fans changed quickly to one of amazement when the *Glance* outperformed all other boats at the Regatta and won thirteen first place prizes in a fourteen race program. Some even suggested that the boat had not been built locally as Rendell and Sexton had claimed. A rumour spread that the boat was actually imported from Halifax and reassembled in St. John's. The Committee was most concerned that if the *Glance* returned for the 1896 Regatta there would be little interest in the races because no boat on the pond could compete with her.

Less than two weeks before the Regatta of 1896 the Committee told Sexton and Rendell that if the *Glance* was entered there would be no Regatta. They explained their concerns and asked that the *Glance* be kept out of the program. To their surprise Rendell agreed. He wanted to demonstrate, however, that the improved style in boat construction would make for better and more competitive races.

Rendell and Sexton sought and received support from the Committee to reconstruct the *Iris,* one of the Phil Mahoney-built boats. In a boathouse at the head of the Pond, Bob Sexton placed the *Iris* on blocks and following Rendell's suggestions, chopped off the bow, stern, and keel and in several days rebuilt the *Iris* as a long boat similar to the *Glance.* Quietly, Rendell arranged for a crew to take the rebuilt *Iris* for a short test run to determine its speed and turning ability.

Regatta Day came and with the *Glance* out of the picture the public expected a more competitive race day. They were again amazed, however, when the Rendell and Sexton rebuilt Iris easily won eleven first place prizes in a fourteen race program. The boat building team of Rendell and Sexton had changed the Regatta forever. Over the following few years, all the old boats were replaced with Bob Sexton-built boats.

SEXTON

When Bob Sexton passed away on July 1, 1944, the *Daily News* referred to him as 'King of the Boat Builders.' While Sam Loveys was perhaps the greatest Regatta boat builder of the nineteenth century, Sexton certainly deserved the recognition given to him at the time of his death by the local media. He had built more Regatta shells than any other builder, and his boats were the fastest in Regatta history. (Nineteen boats according to the *Daily News*, July 31, 1946.) In the period from 1897 to 1944 Sexton, according to press reports of 1944, built all but two of the Regatta boats of that period.

Sexton was born at Bonavista in 1859. He was a fisherman until moving to St. John's in the early 1880s when he accepted work with Lawrence Brothers Carriage Builders who operated from their premises on Gower Street. He quickly earned respect as a craftsman. The *Daily News* commented that as, "...a craftsman in woodwork his skill amounted almost to genius."

RENDELL

Part of Sexton's early success as a boat builder was shared with a fellow boat racing enthusiast Dr. H.H. Rendell. After returning to St. John's from medical school, Dr. Rendell took up yachting (term used for sailing in those days). He also tried canoeing and got more than one ducking during his efforts on Long Pond.

Rendell built his own yacht and named it *Elsie* but it had design defects. He then took a five-week course on the ten-ton *Yawl* where he learned to handle boats. His love for boating led him to a close friendship with Sexton and together the two built some of the best boats ever to compete at the St. John's Regatta.

In 1889 Dr. Rendell and Bob Sexton built a sailing boat which they called *Elsie II*. The two included a lead keel cast and according to one newspaper, "The Wiseacres said they spoiled a good craft. But the Doctor proved the value of outside ballast as against ballast on board." In the sailing races that year *Elsie II* won all the races and earned its owner prizes including a gold medal and a gold cup which were presented by the Honourable A. W. Harvey.

Dr. Rendell teamed up with Bob Sexton in designing new boats for the Regatta, but after the launching of the *Doctor* in 1903, left the boat-building entirely to Sexton and devoted his time fully to his medical practice. All subsequent boats built by Sexton were based on the design of *Blue Peter*.

Rendell had a keen interest in the Regatta and often participated in the yacht-sailing races at Quidi Vidi. His first Regatta effort was the successful remodeling of the *Myrtle* (used by Outer Cove in 1885 to make the 9:20 record that lasted until 1901). Rendell then teamed up with Sexton and designed a new race boat which Sexton built and placed on the Pond in time for the 1895 Regatta. That boat was christened the *Glance*. This marked the beginning of a life-time association with the Quidi Vidi Regatta for Sexton.

* In fact, only three boats were not built by Sexton in this period. They were *Shamrock*, built by a Mr. O' Rourke; *Shananditti*, by Father Pat O' Brien, Bay

Bulls; and *Lady McCallum* by Mr. Mallard of Quidi Vidi.

RENDELL AND SEXTON TEAM UP

Most of the Sexton boats were built at the Lawrence premises and carried to the Pond on the shoulders of rowing crews. Sexton also built and repaired boats at the Academia Boathouse at the head of the Pond and in his back yard on Colonial Street. The exact number of boats designed by Rendell is not known but he did design *Glance, Cabot, Red Cross, Blue Peter, Doctor, Toga,* and *Bob Sexton.* He based his design for the *Blue Peter* on a popular racing shell of the nineteenth century — the *Daisy.* Rendell was so well known by his nickname 'The Doctor' that in 1903 a boat developed by Sexton and Rendell was called after Rendell using this nickname.

Throughout his boat building career, Sexton built more than twenty shells and improved or repaired many others. Bob Sexton's boat building career developed as follows:

1. *Glance* 1895
2. Redesign *of Myrtle* (formerly the *Terra Nova*) . . . 1896
3. *Bob Sexton* 1899
4. *Red Cross* 1900
5. *Blue Peter* 1901
6. *Doctor* 1903
7. *Sam Slick* (renamed *Toga*) 1904
8. *Red Lion* 1906
9. *Nina* 1908
10. *Pink-Un* (Name later changed to *Mary*) 1909
11. *Guard* 1910
12. *Nellie R* 1912
13. *Cadet* 1914

14. *Blue Peter II*. 1925
(Outer Cove were the first to use *Blue Peter II* at the invitation of its owner, the Star of the Sea Association.)

15. *Red Cross* (four-oar). 1936

16. *Royalist* (four-oar) 1936

17. *Coronet* (four-oar) 1937
(Sexton was seventy-eight years old at this time and still active. The four-oared boats were used at the Mundy Pond Regatta 1946 and after.)

18. *Cabot*. . . . . ?

19. *Glance*. 1895

20. *Eclipse* . . . . ?
(All built for Bell Island Regatta.) He also built four boats for the Mundy Pond Regatta.

1922 Championship Race. Outer cove in *Cadet* with a time of 9:40.

In 1925 a Mr. Carberry assisted Bob Sexton in building *Blue Peter II*. He likely assisted in the building of other boats but to date I have not found other references to him. At the age of eighty-four, Sexton was still working on boats and attending Regattas. He remodeled his own yacht in which he spent many happy hours sailing out of St. John's Harbour. He also built, that same year, a seventeen foot sail boat for his employer. Sexton, the King of Boat Builders, continued to work at his craft right up to days before he passed away July 1, 1944.

GENIUS BUILDER

One of the most fascinating stories of Regatta boat-builders involves Bob Sexton. In 1887 his close friend Dr. Rendell, relying on his knowledge of rowing, designed a boat similar to those used in English competitions and showed the model to the City Boat Club. In those days, the boat clubs and not the Committee purchased and owned the race boats. Rendell convinced the City Boat Club of the superiority of this design over those of the Mahoney and Loveys style race-shells. The Club ordered one which they intended to use at the Regatta on Quidi Vidi Lake.

Rendell turned to his friend Bob Sexton to build the new boat. The two met often at each other's homes to plan its construction. Sexton, however, was unable to read blue-prints. To communicate the fine details of his design, the Doctor laid out his plan on a kitchen table using hair pins. Soon after Sexton built a shed in his Colonial Street garden and began to build the boat. As Sexton worked on the design, he saw ways to improve upon it. Sexton interrupted his work to build a new design based on Rendell's original but included his own adjustments and changes. When he went to compare the two designs, he discovered that he had mistakenly destroyed the Rendell model.

Relying on his memory of the hair-pin kitchen table plan laid out by Rendell, Sexton proceeded to build the boat which was later purchased by the City Club and entered in the Regatta. Years later when describing the remarkable boats built by Sexton, Dr. Rendell noted that Sexton built new race boats without any mechanical aid. He had no means to bend timber nor any steam box to aid in bending the long, thin, fragile planks of cedar.

END OF THE SEXTON ERA

The Sexton era ended in 1947, and between 1947 and 1974 four different sets of boats were purchased by the Regatta Committee. None met the quality of the Sexton racers. After Sexton's death, the Committee turned to the Salter Brother's of Oxford, England, who were famous as boat-builders for the Royal Henley. The Salter's-built boats went on the pond in 1948. They were cumbersome and heavy and the fastest time recorded in that period was made by the Waterford Hospital crew when they won the 1951 Championship in the time of 10:27.2. Among the complaints against the Salter Boats was that the seats were not wide enough and the stretchers were not the proper length. The Salter or Oxford Boats that succeeded the Sexton-built boats in 1948 measured forty-eight 1/2 feet long and weighed 380 pounds.

These were replaced in 1952 by the Kelowna Boats (built at Kelowna, British Columbia). The Kelowna's did not compare well with the Sexton boats but race times improved. In 1958, for the first time in ten years, a race time was recorded in less than ten minutes. (William Summers crew 9:58 in Trades Race; Royal Newfoundland Constabulary in Police-Firemen's Race-9:46; and the RNC winning the Championship race in 9:45.) When the Kelowna Boats were replaced in 1962, they were sent for use in the Placentia Regatta.

In 1962 and again in 1967, the Regatta purchased boats built by Richard Simms a Newfoundlander living and working in Toronto. He built the *Miss India*, the *Miss CJON*, the *Royalist* and the *Blue Peter V*. Most crews did not want to use the *Royalist* because they considered it to be inferior to the others. The Simms Shells of 1962 measured fifty-two feet long and weighed 450 pounds. These were longer but lighter than the Kelowna built boats of 1952 which measured fifty and a half feet long and weighed 370 pounds.

The boats used have changed a great deal since the Sexton era. Sexton used oak, pine, elm, and cedar to build his boats. Although, Southside Hills are no longer pine-clad, the Hills were once a source of pine trees. Thirteen of Sexton's boats were forty-nine feet long and two, the *Doctor* and the *Toga* were fifty-one feet long. Sexton imported Spanish Cedar to build the Pink-Un (renamed the Mary) in 1909 because local wood was not available. This contributed to the *Pink-Un* being lighter than the previous Sexton boats. The *Terra Nova* built by Phil Mahoney weighed 800 pounds.

In 1991 and in 1994 new race boats were built by Hudson Boat Works of Komoka, Ontario. They weighed 385.94 pounds. Hudson used Mahogany and Douglas Fir. The Hudson Shells are 50.5 feet long; 2.44 wide and 13.37 inches in depth.

FOUR- AND SIX-OARED RACES

Sporadically throughout Regatta history both four-oar and six-oar races were part of the program. In the first years of Regatta history the same boat was used for both competitions with only the number of rowers changing. In later years specially designed four-oared boats were used. Such was the case in the 1930s and 1940s. The

Committee revived the use of the four-oared competition because of the dwindling interest in the Regatta and the difficulty to attract full crews for the six-oared races. These Regattas held two championship races. The four-oared championship was called the All-Star or four-oared All-Comers Race while the six-oar championship race was called the All-Comers six-oared race. Prior to 1940, crews were allowed to pick rowers from the banks for the All-Comers Race but this practice stopped in 1941. In 1944 there were eight, four-oared races and only four, six-oared races on the Regatta Day Program.

The Regatta tradition carries on early 1970s

CHAPTER SEVEN

The Royal Influence

We Remember well the year,
when the Prince of Wales was here,
when a picked crew from the Hero came
to face us.
But before they reached the stake,
they were beaten half the Lake,
by our fishermen who rowed there at the
Races.

Terra Nova Regatta Program, 1898
author probably Johnny Burke

ROYALTY AND THE REGATTA

Horses may be the sport of kings but the Quidi Vidi Regatta attracted its share of royalty, and over the years, was often influenced and encouraged by royalty. The first royal visitor to the Quidi Vidi Regatta was Prince Henry of the Netherlands. The Prince was expected to arrive for the two-day Regatta which was scheduled for August 7 and 8, 1845. However, as the Frigate *Rhine*, which carried the Prince, neared St. John's Harbour it became engulfed in fog and went astray. Three days later, on August 9, the *Rhine* arrived in St. John's Harbour. Because the Prince expressed disappointment over not being here in time for the races, officials organized a second Regatta. This Regatta was held on Tuesday, August 19 at St. John's Harbour.

Members of the various local societies and bands escorted the Prince from the Harbour to Government House. To welcome the Prince to the city, crowds, some in carriages, gathered along Queen's Wharf and Cochrane Street up to Government House. At Government House a triumphant arch was erected.

THE PRINCE OF WALES

The second royal visit to the Quidi Vidi Regatta was in 1860 when the Prince of Wales, who was later to become King Edward VII of England, enjoyed a day at the Regatta. The monarchy was held in such high esteem that an enterprising gentleman was able to sell seats along the route to give people a good view of the Prince. John Woods constructed a stand of seats that could accommodate 200 people. This was built at the foot of Cochrane Street. Woods charged five shillings for adults and two shillings-six pence for children.

The Prince was taken in a Victoria carriage around the Lake amid repeated cheers from the crowds. He was obviously pleased by the reception and commented that it was worth the several weeks crossing the Atlantic to view such a splendid scene. A Newfoundland Dog was presented to the Prince on behalf of the Newfoundland people. The dog, who was purchased from Newfoundland Dog breeder Bart Sullivan, wore a silver chain from Tiffany's in New York, with an ornamental centre piece surrounded by a wreath of oak leaves. His name was Avalon, but the Prince changed it to Cabot.

The Prince stopped his carriage at Jocelyn's Cottage on the north side of the Pond and chatted with race fans. He then rode horseback to Signal Hill. At a ball held in his honour that night he danced until 3 a.m. Before leaving he donated 100 pounds sterling to be used as prize money for a fishermen's race between St. John's and Harbour Grace to be held on August 26; his father's birthday. It seems that race was never held. In its place, an annual prize for the Derby Day Fishermen's Race was established, and called the 'Prince of Wales Prize.'

A GIFT FOR THE PRINCE OF WALES

One of the gifts presented to the Prince at the 1860 Regatta was a painting by John Hayward; a rower participant in the Regatta. The painting showed the Prince and his dog Cabot. Hayward rowed in the boat called the *Prince of Wales* that year along with Sir James Winter. He had moved to California to live but returned to St. John's in 1911. Hayward wrote a letter to the *Telegram* in which he claimed the painting was still on display at Buckingham Palace at that time. Hayward had been employed as a bookkeeper with the Commercial Bank at St. John's before moving to live in the United States.

In 1992 I contacted the Surveyor of the Queen's Pictures at Buckingham Palace, Charles Noble, enquiring about the picture. Mr. Noble replied that he had made an exhaustive search of Royal Family art works but could find no record of the Newfoundland painting. He also noted that after the Prince died his personal letters written to his mother while abroad had been destroyed.

ANOTHER PRINCE VISITS

The third royal visit to the Regatta was in 1919 and was marred by a tragedy that claimed the life of a popular rower. Larger than usual crowds had gathered at lakeside on Wednesday, August 13, to get a glimpse of His Royal Highness the Prince of Wales. The weather however was less than desirable. The winds were high enough to slow the crews and good times were not being made.

The Prince remained at the Regatta until 10:30 a.m. which was long enough to witness one race. After he left, the winds began to increase, and by 12:30 p.m. there was quite a lop on the pond. Near 1 p.m. the Mercantile Race got underway with Bowrings in the *Guard*, Jobs in the *Cadet,* and Reids in the *Nellie R.*

While turning the buoys, the *Guard* and *Nellie R* began taking on water. The *Guard* moved near shore to bail out water. Before resuming the race two oarsmen left the boat because they felt it would be too dangerous to continue. The *Guard* went on to win the race with a time of 10:52. Aubrey Wight, who later became President of the Regatta Committee, rowed in the *Guard* that day.

Nellie R was not as fortunate. A high and heavy wind struck and swamped the boat. Coxswain Shoddy Rogers attempted to calm the crew. Despite his efforts several crew members panicked. Jim Kent was the first to dive into the water and tried to swim to shore. He was followed by L. Morrissey and T. Bell. Bell held onto the boat.

Crew members Charles Peters, a Sergeant with the Royal Newfoundland Regiment, followed the others. But after diving into the water he failed to come to the surface. Witnesses recalled that Peters made no effort to swim and speculated he may have suffered a heart attack. Meanwhile Rogers, W. Brown, and W. Bemister remained in the sinking boat.

Rogers told the stroke he could keep the boat afloat by turning the oars upright and leaving them in the water. The Committee had two motorless rescue boats at the end of the Pond. Although they were slowed down by the winds, they managed to rescue the men who had remained with the boat.

Meanwhile, Jim Crotty, a Committee member, tossed his coat and vest aside and swam out to Morrissey to help him to shore. A spectator passed Crotty a long piece of board and he went out again into the water. This time he extended the board to Kent, who grabbed it and was pulled to safety. While this tragedy was unfolding, people at the head of the Pond had no idea what was happening. A gloom was cast over the event when the crowds learned of the tragedy. The Committee met and decided to cancel the races.

Prime Minister Sir Michael Cashin and Sir John Crosbie led an attempt to recover Charles Peters' body. The search was called off at 5 p.m. due to heavy rain. The search resumed the next day and the body recovered at 7 a.m. All remaining races were held a week later. Weather conditions were excellent and Logy Bay rowing in the *Cadet* covered the course in 9:32.2.

ROYAL REGATTAS

Our ties with the British Monarchy were often reflected at Regatta time. The Regatta of 1887 was called the Jubilee Regatta in honour of Queen Victoria's Jubilee. Mr. S.O. Steele, owner of the Mercantile House in St. John's, gave out 750 handsome Jubilee Medals to spectators at Lakeside.

The Regattas of 1902 and 1937 were called Coronation Regattas to honour the coronation of English Monarchs. In 1936 City Council, then the only elected body in Newfoundland, made Quidi Vidi Lake area a National Park and called it King George V Park as a memorial to the King.

The Monarchial influence was again felt during WWII. The Regatta had been suspended in 1940 because of the war and was not expected to resume until its end. However, the King of England, in an inspiring message to the Commonwealth, urged people to continue life as normally as possible. In response the Regatta was revived in 1941.

ROYAL GIFTS

After the Lord Warden gold medals were won by the Smith-Stockley crew in 1981, John Perlin approached the Queen Mother, who was then the Lord Warden of the Cinque Ports, to ask if she would replace the famed Lord Warden's Medals (purchased with a donation in 1910 from Lord Brassey, Lord Warden of the Cinque Ports). This she did by providing two sets of her eightieth birthday crowns. Again in 1991 at the request of John Perlin the Queen Mother donated a set of her ninetieth birthday crowns to be awarded to the crew breaking the course record.

The Queen Mother Elizabeth on her 1965 Royal Visit to St. John's. Author Jack Fitzgerald shown here with the Queen Mother on the Royal Yacht *Britannia* during that visit.

QUEEN ELIZABETH II VISITS

The year 1978 marked the first time in Regatta history that a reigning British monarch, Queen Elizabeth II, attended the St. John's Regatta. To accommodate the royal visit Regatta Day was changed to Thursday, July 27. This marked the second consecutive year for a July Regatta. The 1977 Regatta was held in July to accommodate the Canada Summer Games. The Committee had an alternate program arranged in case weather caused a postponement. Eighteen crews had agreed to row, regardless of conditions while the Queen was at Lakeside, "...even if they only row half the distance."

General Earl Haig and Regatta President W.J. Higgins at the 1924 St. John's Regatta. Photo courtesy of City of St. John's Archives.

ANDY WELLS NOT IMPRESSED!

Andy Wells, then a St. John's City Councillor, refused to attend a luncheon for the Queen at City Hall, "...to protest that the ordinary citizens of St. John's were not represented on the elitist guest list." Wells felt the Mayor should have arranged for the Queen to meet a cross section of the city's people. Wells stated, "Anyway, I'm too much of a democrat and an anti-elitist to take these things too seriously." The Royal Visit attracted bigger than usual crowds to Lakeside, and the press estimated attendance was at 50,000 which was the largest ever.

CHAPTER EIGHT

Liquor History of the Regatta

When the rum and ginger beer,
your poor sinking heart to cheer,
sure you'd never lose your head
but take things coolly.
And the whiskey is so mild
you may give it to a child
they'd call it lemonade in Bally Haly.

Johnny Burke's
Regatta Program, 1898

LIQUOR CONSUMPTION

The Regatta survived its beginnings in the 1820s despite disease, a poor economy, and two world wars. Yet the most consistent and challenging factor to its survival was none of the above. From its beginnings in the early 1820s, liquor and rowdiness sparked strong opposition to the Day of the Races and forced its cancellation in many years. Throughout the entire nineteenth century the presence of liquor at lakeside on Regatta Day remained a serious threat to its existence.

During the 1820s when the Quidi Vidi Regatta started, the island of Newfoundland had a population of 20,000 people with 6,000 living in St. John's. Liquor was a major part of life as evidenced by the fact that in just one year during the 1820s, 220,000 bottles of rum were consumed by the Newfoundland population. This did not include brandy, gin, wine, and beer which were also available.

The Bunch of Grapes, owned by a Mr. Best, was a tavern favourably located for early Regattas at Bulley's Farm on the North Side of Quidi Vidi Lake. In that era, the City with a relatively small population, had thirty-three taverns with names as colourful as Tar for all Weather, Rose and Crown, Britannia, the Calibogus Club, and the London Tavern where the first Regatta Committee meetings were sometimes held. In addition to the Bunch of Grapes tavern, liquor patrons often brought their own brews to lakeside on Regatta Day. Because of this it was very difficult to control abuse of liquor during the first years of Regatta history.

LADIES BOYCOTT

The first Regattas held in the 1820s were looked forward to enthusiastically by the menfolk of the city. However, the ladies were not as pleased with the new social and sporting event. In 1828 the women of St. John's attracted some public attention by boycotting the Regatta.

The *Newfoundlander* offered an explanation of the boycott following the Regatta. It reported,

> We feel assured it was just a retaliation on their part for the inattention with which they have been treated for the last 3 or 4 years; and certainly, they could not adopt a more effectual mode of punishment than by absenting themselves from every scene of amusement and proving to the beaus how joyless and dim such pleasure, when not enlivened by their smiles, but that, 'Whether sunn'd in the tropics, or chill'd at the pole; if woman be there, there is happiness too.' We would strongly recommend the ladies until a proper return be made for all their kindness to persevere in this line of conduct and they will soon be able to dictate their own terms.

And what distracted the men from the women at the 1826 and 1827 Regattas? Early records show heavy betting heightened interest in the boat races and there was excessive consumption of, "...the national." (Rum.) Little wonder the ladies felt ignored.

DAMPENED SPIRITS

The use of liquor at the Races often dampened the enthusiasm of many. The Regatta which had been started to relieve summer boredom became a widely anticipated festive season. Men would go on drinking binges that often lasted for a week or more after Regatta Day. This inspired strong opposition from several groups. First, many businessmen opposed the Regatta because labourers failed to return to work and delays were experienced in unloading cargo ships. Housewives joined in the opposition because when husbands went on binges, families were left without money and food until the men sobered enough to return to work. The third source of opposition came from temperance groups who organized all opponents of the Regatta.

Following the 1845 Regatta, opposition was strong enough to put an end to the Regatta. At least it seemed that way. But those who favoured the summer Regatta battled to restore it. Their efforts paid off and in 1851 the Regatta was revived. The Races continued until 1860 but were again cancelled for reasons that included fear of liquor abuses and violence. From 1860 to 1870 no Regattas were held at Quidi Vidi. However boat races were held on St. John's Harbour in 1865. The political and economic uncertainty of the 1860s and the violence associated with it caused authorities to become concerned over continuing a Regatta. It was felt that a public gathering of this magnitude combined with the liquor abuse and rowdyism that went with it could spark violence.

MORE PROBLEMS

Once again, public interest in reviving the Regatta succeeded and the races resumed with enthusiasm in 1871. By 1875 opposition was again mounting against a Regatta. An article in the *Newfoundlander* during August 1875 referred to drunkenness and rowdyism at Lakeside and stated, "...viewed in this light is felt that, however desirable an occasional break in our work-a-day monotony, it is made to cost too dearly and hard though it seems, had better be avoided than purchased at the price of such consequences." In 1877 the same newspaper called upon authorities to increase the number of police at the Regatta and to restrict the number of liquor licences.

Drunkenness and rowdyism were not just spectator vices. At the 1881 Regatta, a drunken Committee member insulted a senior citizen inside the Committee Tent. Some rowers publicly demanded that in the future, sobriety and courtesy be requirements in selecting Committee members. Sometimes little respect was shown towards the police officers on duty Regatta Day. One newspaper reported in August 1885 that an ordinarily well mannered longshoremen, "...had the audacity to place Constable Pynn in a horizontal position." When Pynn recovered, the drunk was taken to the lock up.

This was followed by several letters in newspapers calling for an end to the Regatta. The problem of gambling at Lakeside often went hand in hand with the abuse of liquor. One letter read, "It's outrageous to see clerks betting $10 and merchants $100 on a single race."

GOVERNOR LOVED IT!

The most prominent advocate for the Regatta in 1886 was Governor Des Voeux. He responded to suggestions that the Regatta be cancelled with his statement,

> I regret very much to hear that there are those that regard this meeting with disfavour. I cannot but think they are completely wrong in their sense of proportion. Some are bound to misbehave in any such gathering.

Sometimes acts of liquor-inspired bravado placed lives at risk. Such was the case in 1890 when a drunken spectator jumped into the Lake and tried to race the *Myrtle* up the Pond. When he got in trouble and began drowning, Constable Jim Fitzgerald dove into the water in full uniform. With hundreds of spectators watching, the police office grabbed the drowning man with one arm and with the other grabbed onto a boat passing by. The boat landed the duo safely on shore amid loud cheering and applause from the crowds.

CONGDON'S SPRUCE BEER!

Spruce beer contained alcohol in the 1890s and in 1894 Johnny Congdon of Lazy Bank (Pleasant Street) had grand plans to make money selling it at the Races. He had carefully brewed four large tubs of spruce beer to sell at Lakeside on Derby Day, as the Regatta was sometimes called. However, on the day before the races poor Congdon suffered a misfortune. While he was at Lakeside constructing his concession tent, his home at Lazy Bank caught fire.

Unable to curtail the flames, his wife bravely decided to sacrifice the beer to save the house. Aided by neighbours she began dumping the four beer tubs over the fire. Needless to say, Congdon wasn't a happy man when he returned home to find his home partly destroyed and his beer supply evaporated. He took a great deal of ribbing from neighbours and friends. To add insult to injury, his neighbour at Lakeside sold spruce beer and erected a sign over the tent which read: "Spruce Beer...good for drinking too!"

FOGARTY

The 1844 Regatta stands out in history, not because of any record-breaking races, but because it was at that event that William Fogarty was killed. Amongst the crowd on the banks of Quidi Vidi that day were Jane Flowers, her husband, Billy Fogarty and Paddy Cowman.

All four had been tipping the bottle and an argument erupted between Fogarty and Mr. Flowers. ·

Fogarty delivered a powerful right fist to Flowers' head, causing him to drop to the ground. As the crowd's attention was diverted from the races on the Pond to the Fogarty-Flowers brawl, Jane came to her husband's defence by throwing a rock at Fogarty. Cowman's fist connected with Fogarty's head around the same time.

Fogarty fell to the ground but did not die immediately. He lingered on for two hours and then passed away. Jane Flowers and Patrick Cowman were arrested and tried in Supreme Court on a charge of manslaughter. At the trial, the two doctors who had attended Fogarty on the day he was killed testified for the defence.

Their evidence surprised the people of St. John's. It showed that neither the punches nor the rock had caused Fogarty's death. According to their evidence, the excitement of the fight had caused blood vessels in his brain to burst. Medical evidence showed that death could not have been caused by the blows because the body was sound and uninjured.

The jury took only twenty minutes to arrive at a 'Not Guilty' verdict. It was a Regatta to remember. The Regatta of 1891 also had a tragic ending. A twenty year old man named Fleming drank too much liquor, fell asleep near the Lake and suffocated. Friends discovered him as people left the area at the conclusion of the Regatta.

POOH BAH'S

In 1904 the Licensing Board which controlled the sale of liquor refused all requests to sell spirits at the Regatta. Some patrons were sufficiently angered by the decision that they sent letters to the newspapers. One person's letter in the *Telegram* stated,

If the board made its decision known two weeks ago, there'd be no Regatta in 1904. There are too many Pooh-Bahs in this country.

sgd. Buttercup
Buttercup was a race boat of the nineteenth century

A second letter said,

Are the people of this country not to be trusted on a race course where liquor is in close proximity without becoming fit subjects for straight jackets?

The law did not prevent some from bringing their own to the races. One such person jumped into the Lake and vowed that he could race the *Blue Peter* up the Pond. He was pulled out by the police.

A verse from Johnny Burke's 1898 program speaks of liquor at the old-time Regattas. He wrote:

And meself was no way shy
for to wet the other eye
and then with rolling gait for home I faces.
And it's many and many a load
I slept off on the road
Oh, the morning of the Terra Nova Races.

SHEBEEN TENTS

During the prohibition years police were always on, "...the Qui Vie for Shebeen Tents." These were bootlegger tents which did a thriving business at Lakeside. To avoid detection they used passwords in order to gain access. Some operators made themselves known only to a selected crowd in order to avoid detection. The Regatta

Committee had a liquor related rule regarding spares during the 1920s and 1930s. All spares had to remain sober...at least until the boats passed the Committee Tent.

With the large numbers of troops coming and going in St. John's during the 1940s it is remarkable how well the liquor problem was controlled. After the 1942 Regatta, a City Magistrate commented on the absence, "...of the usual run of drunks." Inspector Case said that not a single arrest had been made at Quidi Vidi. Yet, the era was not without incident.

St. John's Regatta 1941. Photo courtesy of *Atlantic Guardian.*

In 1945 an American sailor inebriated on home brew rolled up his sleeves and challenged one and all to fisticuffs. He was doing well until he came up against a fellow named Bradbury from Torbay, "...a giant of a man who quickly disposed of his adversary."

COMMITTEE SCANDAL

During the 1950s a scandal developed relating to the Regatta Committee's fund raising efforts. The scandal was uncovered after cheques made payable to the Committee were found blowing around Lakeside. Some of the funds collected found its way into the pockets of two of the fund raisers who spent much of the cash getting drunk. The Committee saw the need to review its fund raising programs and consequently tightened them up. It was John Perlin, a former President of the Regatta Committee and Regatta Hall of Fame Member, who devised the system of issuing receipts and land use permits.

Although the problem of theft was effectively dealt with, the tradition of Committee members bringing liquor into the Higgins Marquee and the boathouse continued until 1978. Queen Elizabeth and the Duke of Edinburgh visited the Regatta that year. John Perlin successfully appealed to Committee members to discontinue the old custom in order to present a show of competence to our royal visitors. Recalling that eventful year, Perlin later commented , "...it was not hard to sell and seemed to be an idea that won instant acceptance." Since 1978, liquor has not been consumed by members on Regatta Day.

BATTLING DRUNKS

Mike Murphy, author of *Pathways to Yesteryear*, was a member of the local Newfoundland Constabulary during the 1930s and often worked a shift on Regatta Day at Lakeside. Reminiscing in the late 1960s about the old time Regattas, Murphy recalled that, "There were times when the annual Regatta at Quidi Vidi Pond was more like a battlefield than anything else. We'd charge in with our night sticks and those drunks would fight right back."

Murphy recalled that police made few arrests in those days. Instead they would take the drunks to a tent where they would sleep it off. On Regatta Day the whole force would be on duty. Today there will be about forty-five constabulary members on duty at lakeside. Their job is mainly traffic and crowd control, as few drunks have been seen at the annual event in recent years.

Early 1900s St. John's Regatta. Photo courtesy of City of St. John's Archives.

Murphy noted that in earlier times,

> They had the hop beer tents and people could get drunk at the Regatta. The hop beer, occasionally flavoured with Beaver tobacco plugs, was pretty potent stuff and the men who drank it were a pretty aggressive bunch. ...belligerent and tough, not like the alcoholics you have today who can barely lift a hand toward you. These men were mean.

He continued,

> When they got out of hand we went at them without clubs. We rarely arrested them but brought them into a tent to sleep it off. They had to be really bad before they were arrested.

Murphy said that sometimes you could tell a fight was "...in the making." He gave as an example the story of the hop beer tent at the head of the pond.

There was one guy who had a hop beer tent right at the head of the pond and every now and then you'd see him run out of the tent, scoop up a bucket of water from the lake and throw it in the beer keg when he got a bit low. This was usually where the trouble broke out.

Murphy concluded,

Also common were the lost kids. There'd be about ten at a time in the police tent all squawking and we'd have to wait for their parents to come for them. ...eventually we'd buy them candy and stuff until they were calmed.

HARRY MURPHY'S VERSE

While recalling old time Regattas, the late Harry Murphy of Flower Hill, who never missed a Regatta and rowed in many, noted there was a tent operated at Lakeside by Sam Haynes. Harry said that Haynes had a verse he made popular by publishing it in one of the Regatta Day Programs (1913). It was simply called, 'Beer.'

Beer is the very best drink on the course.
Beer is the drink when from barking you're hoarse.
It cures indigestion and all inward pains.
Drop in for a bottle and ask for Sam Haynes.

In those days children sang the following verse which summed up some of the old-time Regattas.

Coming home from the races,
Bleeding noses and cut faces,
and we're all as drunk as blazes,
Coming home from the Pond.

CHAPTER NINE

Inspirations

Bless the Regatta that brought us together,
Big men and little men, short men and
tall.
Some from the seaside and some from the
heather.
City men, Country men — but Oarsmen
all!

From Frank 'Spotty' Baird Collection

THE REGATTA INSPIRES

Each decade produces outstanding people who excel in a sport or profession and whose achievements survive to inspire later generations. Regatta history is filled with such people and it would take volumes to chronicle them all. This chapter deals with some of the earlier legendary figures who, by their example and successes, contributed to the longevity and success of the Royal St. John's Regatta.

The fishing community of Outer Cove produced some of the most outstanding rowers and crews of the nineteenth and early twentieth centuries. Blackhead, with just six families, produced the second strongest crew in 100 years. The community of Torbay also played a major role in the success of the Regatta.

In the first half of the twentieth century, the West End Police helped revitalize the Regatta with a string of successes and they were followed by a teenage crew known as the Higher Levels that won two championships. Both the police and teenagers inspired crews for the next several decades.

DICK SQUIRES

The Regatta of 1874, held on Thursday, August 6, is best remembered for the controversial scull race which injured the pride of Newfoundland oarsmen and led to a challenge match two weeks later on Quidi Vidi. The weather was less than ideal and inspired the following comments by a reporter for the *Times*:

> Notwithstanding unpleasant indications of weather, the glorious orb of day looking quite 'sickly' and intense fog peering o'er yonder hills. A little rain fell

to the great discomfort of silks and satins…beauty and fashion; and which indeed gave a cheerless aspect to the whole.

This year's Committee chairman was Dr. J.J. Dearin. Out of the twelve races held, seven were four-oared whaleboats, jolly boats and ship gigs; four were six-oared whaleboats; and the final one was the single scull race.

The centre of attraction was the scull race because skippers of several Nova Scotian vessels in port persuaded the Nova Scotia scull champion George Ferguson to participate. This matching of Newfoundlanders against a foreigner stirred local patriotism and increased interest in Derby Day. Heavy betting took place at Lakeside and the Ferguson backers put a lot of money on the scull race.

The race was not as competitive as expected and Ferguson was an easy winner. The win, however, injured the pride of local oarsmen and controversy about the handling of the race spilled over into the local press. Some complained that the St. John's oarsmen were at a disadvantage because they were already exhausted after having rowed two contests in the afternoon. They charged that the Committee had wrongly forced the men to row in a state of fatigue. On the other hand, they pointed out Ferguson was a skilled oarsman with sculls and had defeated several champion oarsmen in foreign waters, and had stepped into his boat "…as fresh as a daisy. He couldn't help but win."

Ferguson defended his victory, claiming that "…some in the City were poor losers." Another local oarsman noted bitterly that Ferguson had lost the scull race in 1873 "…but defeat under the circumstances they procured it, is infinitely preferable to the ignoble victory they (Ferguson) have won." (He was referring to a challenge race the previous year which Ferguson had lost.

Challenge races did not necessarily take place on Regatta Day.)

With bitter feelings riding high, a small advertisement appeared in the *Times*. Richard Squires, plain, of Broad Cove (St. Phillips) issued a challenge to George Ferguson to meet him in a scull race at Quidi Vidi. Squires suggested a purse for the winner of between fifty and one hundred dollars. He concluded the ad stating, "If the challenge is not accepted today, business will require me to leave town for my home."

Ferguson accepted the challenge and a match was set for Saturday, August 22, at 4 p.m. The controversy had fanned public sentiment and thousands lined the banks of 'ye olde Kitty Vitty' to witness the contest between a Newfoundlander and a foreigner. At stake for them was not just the winning of a race but their national pride. Ferguson's supporters were there too and betting was heavy.

Describing the scene at Quidi Vidi, the *Times* reported:

> Even Cleopatra, when she reclined in her silken gondola on the water of beautiful Venice was never more highly elevated or honoured than was Terra Nova's son, plain Richard Squires of Broad Cove on the afternoon of Saturday last, when after having proved the victor in the challenge scull race on Quidi Vidi Lake, he was at once declared to be entitled to the belt. ...taken possession of himself and boat, and heartily conveyed through the town on the shoulders of the bone and sinew of Newfoundland; led by a band of music and an immense assemblage of people old and young from extreme exultation; knew not whether they were on their heads or their heels.
>
> When Squires took his seat in the boat on the Pond he seemed to be quite confident of success. He was nerved for the combat and as cool as the cucum-

ber of the good host and hostess whose popular and much frequented cottage breasts the lake.

The *Times* went on to state,

> Mr. Ferguson who had accepted the challenge, prudently gave up the contest when he found that his opponent was one too many for him. But, nevertheless, took all in good part and on landing warmly shook hands with Squires. Squires received a capital purse for the benefit of himself and his family.

Our local oarsmen and supporters couldn't miss the opportunity to gloat over the win. One penned a letter to the press claiming that one of the women of Outer Cove was preparing to challenge Ferguson and would put up a 1,000 pound purse. The boats in that race would be called the *Sculpin* and the *Muskrat*, the letter noted, and continued, "She'll wear the 'fanny bloomer costume' trimmed with green, a la mode, while George will be attired in blue." He suggested a band be present to serenade the Nova Scotia captains who backed Ferguson. Some of the songs he expected they would play included:

1) Pulling Hard Against the Stern;
2) Captain Horse and the Jinx Marines;
3) I Couldn't Help Laughing;
4) Riding in a Boat;
5) My Gondola's Waiting Below, Dear;
6) How Is That For I;
7) Wait for the Tide to Turn; and
8) Banks of Newfoundland.

The letter was signed "Gosling."

JOHN COAKER

In 1885 another legendary Challenge Race was set that awakened the patriotic spirit of Newfoundlanders. This time another Halifax resident, Thomas Leahy, challenged a man named John Coaker. The outcome of the race made Regatta history and the prowess of Johnnie Coaker remained famous down through the years.

When Coaker had first rowed in 1882 he was beaten by local resident Allan Barnes. He was back the following year and won an easy victory against four other oarsmen, including Barnes. The Regatta of 1885 was held on August 5 and for many days thereafter there was a growing desire to bring about a race between Coaker and Leahy. A large attendance for the event was assured.

In issuing the challenge, Leahy had written to Coaker saying he did not wish to row the race on paper, and concluded with the threat, "If I do not hear from you definitely by Thursday at noon, I will conclude you intend to rest on your laurels until next season." Coaker had little choice but to accept; how could any Newfoundlander be belittled in 1885 by a Canadian, especially at his own game — rowing?

The race was set for the last day of August at 5:00 p.m. However, a sudden breeze came up and it was postponed until half past six, at which time "the breeze had exhausted itself and only the tiniest wavelets danced and sparkled in the rays of the setting sun." During the waiting period, interest continued to mount and Leahy's followers, present in full force, began placing bets on a two-to-one basis on their now over-confident fellow countryman. At the same time they continued to praise him and to "display their mature judgement and experience on aquatic matters in general." They had obviously forgotten the lesson of 1874 when Squires of Broad Cove had rowed Ferguson out of recollection, so to speak.

Prudence was thrown to the wind and up to race time they continued to revel with great pride in the ability of their own Thomas Leahy.

At 6:31 p.m. sharp, the gun was fired and both men were off. The course rowed was two and one-half miles. They started at the lower end of the lake, came up and went down again and then back once more for the finish. As the two left the starting line, a bellowing cry went up from the supporters on the bank. At first the boats seemed neck and neck but Coaker pulled ahead. He started with about thirty-five strokes to the minute; Leahy was much slower. But at the buoys they were again tied. At this point a 'perfect frenzy' prevailed, "...the crowd yelling their delight, waving their hats recklessly, running about and doing all manner of ridiculous things, in their excitement." Before both men came halfway down the Pond, however, it was evident Coaker was running away with it as Leahy began to tire. At the buoy it was Coaker by three boat lengths, then five, then ten, until finally at the end he had beaten the foreigner by twenty boat lengths. The time, nineteen minutes five seconds.

When the hero came ashore he was seized by those on the bank and, as in the case of Squires, was placed in his boat and carried on the shoulders of 100 stalwarts to his home on Southside. A brass band accompanied the triumphant marchers, followed by thousands of race fans.

The man who they had claimed was afraid to row the Pond, John Coaker, was proclaimed a local hero and went on to become a City Councillor in St. John's.

THE PLACENTIA CHALLENGE

Less than fifteen years after the famous Placentia Giants came to St. John's and won the Fishermen's Race, rowers from St. John's attempted to repay Placentia by bringing race boats to that community in hope of beating its rowers. It was in 1891 that the Total Abstinence Society took two boats from Quidi Vidi to Placentia for a rowing showdown. The boats used were the *Iris* and the *Gypsy*.

Crowds turned out to witness the race held on the north side of Placentia. Rowing for St. John's in the *Iris* were the St. John's Tradesmen, while a crew from Placentia rowed in the *Gypsy*.

This race attracted attention for several reasons. First, the St. John's rowers were hoping to accomplish in Placentia what Placentia had accomplished in St. John's when they brought a boat to Quidi Vidi and were victorious on the Lake. The second reason was that the *Gypsy* and *Iris* were considered top notch boats of equal speed and they had raced to a dead heat at Quidi Vidi in a challenge race that year.

Placentia humbled the St. John's rowers by defeating them, but they were splendid hosts to the T. A. Party and treated them to lunch and entertainment that evening.

DEAD HEATS

Regatta history records four dead heats. The first took place in 1886 during a Challenge Race when the St. John's crew tied with a Fishermen's crew from Torbay. A second dead heat took place in 1891 between the *Iris* and the *Gypsy*. The third in 1900 was a thrilling race all the way that saw the *Glance* and the *Bob Sexton* race to a dead heat. The time in that race was 9:55.8. In 1974 the Championship Race became the fourth dead heat and the first Championship to end in a dead heat. In that race Hickmans and Newfoundland Light and Power covered the course in 10:10.2 with both crews sharing the Championship honours.

RECORDS

The community of Outer Cove produced the finest rowers ever to compete in the Regatta. In addition to the famous 9:13 record of 1901, they held several nine-teenth century records including the achievement of recording the most consecutive years with the fastest time of the day. That record covered the five years from 1883 to 1887. The award for the best time of the day was the Governor's Cup. In addition to winning the Cup for five consecutive years they were considered Champions for five consecutive years.

1883, *Volunteer* 9:45
1884, *Volunteer* 10:13
1885, *Myrtle* 9:20
1886, *Myrtle* 9:35
1887, *Avalon* 9:40

Both Outer Cove records were tied by the West End Police crew between 1935 and 1939 by winning the Governor's Cup and Championship for those five con-secutive years:

1935, *Star of the Sea* 9:47
1936, *Blue Peter* 10:12
1937, *Star of the Sea* 9:41
1938, *Coronet* 9:37.5
1939, *Coronet* 9:46.8

The Governor's Cup was awarded to the crew with the fastest time of the day.

The West End Police crew of the 1930s ranks among the top ten crews of Regatta History. Their strong performance on the Pond renewed enthusiasm for the Regatta which had been waning in the 1930s. In addition, they were an inspiration and model crew for generations of rowers to follow. The Police recorded a race time in 1938 that remained the best time on the Pond for forty-three years. They tied the record set by Outer Cove for the most consecutive championship wins. The West End Police also share with Outer Cove and the William Summers crew the record for the most consecutive years recording the best time of the day.

One hundred and twenty-three races took place at Regattas during the 1930s. The ten minute barrier was broken only on twenty-four occasions and by a variety of fishermen and labour crews. According to newspapers, the Police Race was introduced for the first time in 1935. In the five years that followed, the West End Police broke the ten minute barrier on seven occasions. In 1938 they rowed the course in 9:37.2 which stood as the best time from 1938 to 1981.

The Police tied the record for the Governor's Cup in 1939 during a race held in near darkness. The Regatta that year started on Wednesday and was postponed due to high winds until Thursday. It did not get underway until 9 p.m. with darkness setting in. The judges couldn't see the boats at times due to the lack of light. The Police finished the race in a time of 9:46.8. The crew was inducted into the Regatta Hall of Fame in 1998.

Members of the West End Police Force included Levi Rogers, cox; Jim Carter, stroke; Tim Gibbons; R. Martin; R. Hillier; J. Nash; and R. Kelland. Tim Gibbons, who had a distinguished rowing career at the Regatta, was the father of the Gibbons brothers of Newfoundland hockey fame: Brian, Sandy, and Gerard.

In 1964 the William Summers crew earned a prominent place in Regatta history by becoming the first crew to win six straight championship races. The Summers crew, however, failed to record the best time of the day in 1964 when they won their sixth straight championship. In that year the best time of the day was 10:00 rowed by the General Hospital crew. Cox for that crew was Cyril Boland, an inductee into the Regatta Hall of Fame.

BLACKHEAD

The Blackhead crew of 1904 stands among the giants of Regatta History. Yet, the memory of that great crew and their achievement has all but faded from public consciousness. Very few people today are even aware that the tiny community of Blackhead ever participated in the St. John's Regatta.

Blackhead was an unlikely community to compete at the Regatta. According to the *Daily News* of August 1904 there were only a half dozen families at Blackhead. Yet for the decade starting with 1904, they sent crews to the races. The Regatta spirit was strong in the community. In those days crews generally did not practice either long or hard. But the rowers from Blackhead would row from their community to Quidi Vidi Harbour. From there they would walk to Quidi Vidi Lake to practice and become familiar with the race course. On Regatta Day the entire community would set out in their fishing boats at 6 a.m. for Quidi Vidi Village. They carried with them a supply of food for a traditional type boil up at Lakeside.

Although, they were few in number, their spirit was obvious on Regatta Day. They provided a strong and loud cheering section for their men, and regularly waded out into the water to greet the crew after they rowed past the finish line.

The small band from Blackhead had much to cheer about on Regatta Day 1904. This was just three years after Outer Cove set the famous 9:13 record. It was the era when Outer Cove and fishing communities like Torbay, Middle Cove, Logy Bay, and Petty Harbour put strong crews in the Regatta.

When the little boats from Blackhead tied up at Quidi Vidi Harbour before 8 a.m. it was overcast and they did not know what to expect from the weather. However, the clouds dispersed, the sun shone brilliantly, and by the time the races started it was an ideal day; similar to Regatta Day 1901, when Outer Cove rowed into history.

Blue Peter — Outercove Fishermen — Quickest Time. 9 m. 13 4-5 s. 1901

As usual betting was heavy at lakeside. The favoured crew in the Fishermen's Race was Outer Cove. Participating in that race were four crews: Blackhead in the *Togo*; Petty Harbour in the *Doctor*; Logy Bay in the *Red Cross*; and Outer Cove in the *Blue Peter*. The next day the *Daily News* reported: "It was generally felt the *Blue Peter* would carry off the Palm and few would bet against her, however; but the victory fell to the *Togo* (Blackhead) which was only considered in the running for second place."

Not only did Blackhead outclass the favourite Outer Cove crew by two boat lengths, they recorded the significant and outstanding time of 9:21.2. Many observers, impressed by the performance of the Blackhead men, suggested they could have beaten the 9:13 record. Coming up the pond, however, their pace slowed as they waved to their supporters on shore. This was an outstanding time even for that period. Most times in that era were in the ten minute range.

However, the true measure of Blackhead's greatness lies in the fact that their time in 1904 remains the second best time recorded on the old race course. Later that Regatta Day, only two crews faced off for a championship race. Outer Cove hoped to regain its lost pride by winning this contest over the crew from Blackhead.

When word spread among spectators that Mike Healy had a sore hand (he had rowed so hard in the Fishermen's Race that his hand bled), the betting again shifted in favour of Outer Cove. There was even some doubt that Blackhead would compete in the championship race. However, press reports the next day showed that the race was not a disappointment. The two crews turned the buoys together and were neck to neck coming up the pond. Blackhead gained a few feet on Outer Cove and maintained this close lead to the finish. For the second time that day, and under trying conditions, Blackhead made another excellent time — 9:24. By the end of the race, according to the newspapers, Healy was suffering excruciating pain.

The victory earned the crewmembers silver medals and each a coat which was donated by the Newfoundland Clothing Company. Members of the crew were A.G.

Williams, cox; M. Healy, stroke; G. Cook; M. Healy; J. Healy; W. Healy; and J. Cook.

In 1905 the competitive spirit was still strong between Blackhead and Outer Cove. These were the only two crews competing in the Fishermen's Race that year and Outer Cove were again the favourites. Yet, Blackhead took the lead from the start and remained a half boat length ahead until turning the buoys. They pulled ahead and won the race by three boat lengths. Their impressive time of 9:40.8 was excellent, even in those days. For this win, the Blackhead crew received gold medals and two dollar gold pieces. The two crews were scheduled to compete in the championship but several Blackhead rowers became ill and the crew withdrew. Outer Cove rowed for time only and recorded a time of 10:30.4.

In 1906, G. Lewis replaced Williams as cox. This time they rowed in the *Red Lion* and again won the Fishermen's Race and recorded the best time of the day — 9:34. The next day, the *Daily News* reported that if Blackhead had been steered better they would have recorded a better time. There was no championship in 1906. It had been on the program but dropped by the Committee.

Blackhead had crews in the Regatta from 1875 until shortly before the start of World War I.

(By 1995 the remarkable rowing achievement of the 1904 rowing crew from Blackhead had been obliterated from public memory. I was pleased to research their story and bring it to the attention of the Regatta Hall of Fame in 1995.)

REVIVED REGATTA

Political and economic turmoil led to the suspension of the Regattas starting in 1861. The Regatta was not revived until 1871 under the leadership of the following gentlemen: John E. Roach, Alan McDougall, Edward Kelley, John Baird, and A.S. Milroy. The following citizens assisted as judges for the event: Capt. T. W. Walters, John Meehan, and Capt. Philip Cleary. The names of the boats which rowed in 1871 included the *John*, *Jeanette*, *Henrietta*, *Hawk*, *Duck*, *Nimrod*, *Elizabeth*, and *Golden Fleece*. These were jolly boats, ship gigs, and pilot boats.

After the decade interlude, the revival of the St. John's Regatta met with a great deal of enthusiasm and strong public support. It was held at Quidi Vidi Lake on Thursday, August 3, and at St. John's Harbour on Sunday, August 6.

The banks at Quidi Vidi were covered with marquees, tents, and flags of many colours. The *Newfoundland Chronicle* described the scene: "Thousands of persons were present at Lakeside and a large number of private and other carriages were filled with fair ladies and gallant gentlemen." In respect to the availability of liquor at Lakeside, the *Chronicle* reported, "...there was a good deal of grog imbibing but the effects were by no means so apparent as might be expected." The newspaper speculated that either there was less drinking at the Races or the liquor was diluted.

Most of the races were in four-oared whaleboats. No times were recorded this year. The winning boats included the *John*, *Hawk*, *Native*, *Fletcher*, *Golden Fleece*, *Lilly* and *Nimrod*. In Regattas of the nineteenth century, emphasis was placed on the boats rather than the crews. Boats were of various sizes and types, and spectators tried to assess the fastest boat by its appearance. Newspaper reports mentioned only the names of the boats and rarely the crews.

Six boats participated in the Harbour Regatta. Starting from Grieve and Co. Wharf at 3:25 p.m., they rowed a course that took them out to and around a boat moored at Chain Rock and back to Grieve's, where the judges witnessed the race from the *Little Nell*. First place went to the *Brackenholm* rowed by Captain Spink; the time was 30:20. The second-place prize went to the *Jane*, rowed by Captain McDougall in thirty-three minutes.

THE 1877 AND 1977 PLACENTIA CREWS

There was much excitement in the city of St. John's in 1877 when it was learned that crews from Placentia and Harbour Grace would be entering the Fishermen's Race at the Regatta.

The local gentry were familiar with the top rowers from surrounding fishing communities, but the prospects of two new fishing crews for the Set Race (Fishermen's Race) stirred a great deal of confusion and uncertainty among those who participated in the widespread gambling.

Outer Cove and Torbay were frequently the fastest crews with the best boats. Now they had to consider the two new rowing crews from far outside the city.

The Regatta of 1877 was held on Thursday, August 9. The deadline for registration was August 8 (Wednesday) but it was extended a day because the Placentia crew were behind schedule arriving in town. They had set out from Placentia late in the afternoon of Saturday, August 4 for St. John's. The boat was loaded aboard a horse drawn sloven for the eight-six mile journey.

Ned Sinnott of Placentia was paid seventy-five dollars by John Foran, a prominent St. John's hotel owner and Regatta Committee member, to build the race boat for the 1877 Regatta. Sinnott put together a strong crew of fishermen and advised Foran that he would be entering a crew to test the speed of the new boat at the Regatta. They were expected to complete their journey to St. John's in three and a half days to meet the August 7 registration date. They failed to arrive by August 7 and registration was extended one day to accommodate them. Placentia made it by August 8 and, after registering, carried the new boat on their shoulders to Quidi Vidi Lake for a practice spin and to get familiar with the race course.

Some Placentia fans, proud of the fact they were sending a crew to the St. John's Regatta, held little hope that they could actually beat a St. John's area fishing crew. On the day the boat left Placentia, a letter was mailed to the *Morning Chronicle* in St. John's which expressed hope that the crew would make a favourable showing in St. John's. The letter signed, "Correspondent" stated, "...it is hard to expect men who have had no practice and who are unaccustomed to the pond to match men like you have in St. John's; well-practiced and acquainted with the race course." He continued, "There is great praise due to Mr. Sinnott for attempting such a thing at all, much more for finishing, in such a manner as he has, the Placentia." At first there was some confusion over the actual name of the boat. The *Chronicle* reporting on the arrival referred to Sinnott's boat as the *Electric*. It stated, "The new race boat *Electric* with her crew arrived from Placentia yesterday morning." The article also identified Ned Sinnott as its builder. The press coverage of the races in which the boat participated referred to it as the *Placentia*. It was later called the *Contest*. Meanwhile, there was a boat in the Regatta named the *Electric Flash*.

Although the story of the 1877 Placentia crew developed legendary proportions, they actually won only one race out of six in which they participated. The race won was the most important one of the day — the

Fishermen's Race (Set Race) in which the best rowers of the Regatta usually participated. They recorded the time of 10:28 in that race which was the best time for the day. The boat itself was considered inferior to others on the pond.

Contrary to legend, when Placentia left the city that night they did not carry the boat back to Placentia on their shoulders. Their trip back was a little easier because they had the horse-drawn sloven exclusively for their own use. With the legend of the Seven Giants set aside, their win that day was impressive because they had travelled a long distance with little opportunity to practice and familiarize themselves with the race course yet succeeded in winning the Fishermen's Race. The Placentia crew of 1877 was inducted into the Regatta Hall of Fame.

On Monday, August 13, 1877, Foran sold the boat for $112 at the Market House in St. John's. In subsequent Regattas, it was called the *Contest* but its performance was not great.

One hundred years later in 1977 a spirited crew from Placentia lead by Adrian O'Keefe paid tribute to the Placentia crew of 1877 by walking to St. John's carrying a race boat and competing in the St. John's Regatta. This time, the Placentia rowers actually carried a race-shell all the way. The 1977 Placentia crew was the defending championship crew at the St. John's Regatta. They had won the 1976 Regatta Championship and had won the Placentia Championship in 1977 before setting out on their historic trek. The crew recorded a 10:18 win in the Labour Race and a 10:56 win in the Transport Race. Even St. John's cheered when the spirited Placentia rowers won the Championship Race in a time of 9:54.2. Members of the crew were Adrian O'Keefe, cox; Tom Whittle, stroke; Anthony Whittle; Gerard

Barron; Brendan Whittle; Leo Collins; and Frank Lannon.

In 1971, O'Keefe, no doubt a Regatta all-time great, showed the type of remarkable enthusiasm for the Regatta that has been its source of strength for almost 200 years. He was the coxswain for the Placentia Juvenile crew at the St. John's Regatta in 1971. The Regatta was postponed from Wednesday to Saturday. This created a problem for O'Keefe because he was scheduled to be married on Saturday.

Not wanting to let his crew down, he left his wedding celebrations and rushed to get to St. John's by 5:50 p.m. for the Juvenile Race. He set out with his wife from Placentia at 4 p.m. in his brother's car. They were accompanied by his wife's sister and her friend. In the excitement of the day his brother neglected to tell him the gas gauge was not accurate. About twenty miles from St. John's the car ran out of gas.

With just thirty-minutes to race time, a car came along and offered assistance. However, they had room for only one person. Adrian left his new bride and the others on the highway with a promise to send help. He got into the car and headed for St. John's.

O'Keefe jumped out of the car when it got caught in a traffic jam near the old Memorial Stadium and ran all-out towards the boathouse. He got there just as his crew was exiting their dressing room. The boys were so happy to see him that they carried him on their shoulders to the boat. Just before the starting gun fired, O'Keefe commented, "Now boys, give me a wedding present. You don't know what I went through to get here." The legendary O'Keefe got his wish and his crew easily won their race.

Now he was able to get on with his wedding day. He picked up some gas and arranged a drive back to the Trans Canada Highway to pick up his bride. He was fortunate to have married a girl who strongly encouraged his love for the Regatta.

SHOTTY ROGERS

Levi 'Shotty' Rogers, who spent fifty-eight consecutive summers with the Annual Regatta at historic Quidi Vidi Lake, was born in St. John's in 1887. Although small in stature, five feet four inches tall and weighing only 115 pounds, Shotty Rogers' first five years with the Regatta were as an oarsman. The remaining fifty-three years were as a coxswain where, during his career, he steered over 300 crews, a record which has never been equalled or beaten and in all probability never will be.

As a builder, Rogers established a legend in the recruiting and training of championship crews for the Regatta. There is hardly a single oarsman who was not influenced either directly or indirectly by Shotty. He steered his last championship crew in 1962 with more than fifty years and over 100 victories to his credit.

In recognition of Levi Shotty Rogers' contributions to Canadian sport, he was inducted, posthumously, into Canada's Sports Hall of Fame in the summer of 1973. A suitable recognition for a distinguished sportsman. (*Daily News*, July 28, 1977)

SHOTTY'S RECORD:
Most Races: approximately 300
Most Wins:158
Most Championships: 19
Most Successive Championships: 8
Most Wins Regatta Day: 7
Longest Years of Service: 53

THE BALLAD OF THE 9:13

The 9:13 had begun to take on legendary proportions in the early 1950s and by 1960, some of the most respected experts at the Regatta were suggesting the record would never be beaten. Among those was a giant of Regatta history Levi 'Shotty' Rogers. Rogers told reporters, "...the 9:13 would never be beaten. The best time we can expect to see is 9:35." He described the ideal crew needed to hit the 9:35, "...as being an average 5'10" height, 170 pounds weight, and they must put in two months training."

Local historian Leo English, O.B.E., recorded the feat of the 1901 Outer Cove crew in the following song:

MEN OF THE 9:13

Come all who love a manly sport a story I will tell,
It's of a famous racing crew that in Outer Cove did dwell.
They were on Quidi Vidi Lake, the finest ever seen,
For they rowed the old *Blue Peter* in the time of 9:13.

Oh, well I do remember boys, that far Regatta time,
With fortune wheels and hop beer carts, and Dobbin in his prime.
With pork and cabbage dinners took, for lunch an old crubeen,
Our bets were done and sweepstakes won, when they made the 9:13.

The morning race for fishermen was taken by Torbay.
These sturdy lads from Outer Cove were grim faced all that day.
They swore they'd win the championship, and revenge full keen,
In Sexton's old *Blue Peter* and a record 9:13.

Now on the crew from Outer Cove John Whalen was the stroke,
John Nugent, two McCarthy boys, Mart Boland and Din Croke.
Walt Power was their coxswain bold, he knew his men I mean,
When he drove her round the course that day in the time of 9:13.

The gun was fired and yellow spray was seen on either hand,

As cheers broke out the band struck up, "The Banks of Newfoundland."
It was nip and tuck right to the stakes with muscles taut and lean.
Our heroes won by half a length in the time of 9:13.

I'm getting old and passing years must bring a fond regret,
For greasy pole and old square dance the things that men forget.
One dying wish when I take off and trip to 'Fiddler's Green,'
They'll ferry souls where Jordan rolls those men of 9:13.

Published *Daily News*, August 1960

Regatta great Skipper Jim Ring who was immortalized in the ballad *The Grand Time of 9:12.04.*

Eighty years later another crew inspired another ballad for a superior performance at the Regatta. The names of Skipper Jim Ring and the Smith-Stockley crew of 1981 are etched in Regatta history forever. Skipper Ring was the inspiration behind the success of the Smith-Stockley crew. In 1981, rowing in the *Native*, the crew rowed the course in 9:12.04. The time was made in the Club Race and the crew went on to win the Championship in the time of 9:23.19.

Members of that crew were Skipper Jim Ring, Cox; Randy Ring, stroke; John Barrington; Tom Power; Brian Cranford; Bill Holwell; and Paul Ring. Tribute is paid to the Smith-Stockley crew in a ballad written in 1981 by Pat Casey called, 'The Grand Time of 9:12.04.' Part of the ballad reflects the high regard held for Skipper Ring:

> So here's good luck to you Skipper,
> May you always have fortune and fame,
> Each year at the grand old Regatta,
> May they always remember your name.
> And when you've advanced to your nineties,
> May pretty girls flock round your bed,
> And may you be settled in heaven before,
> The devil finds out that you're dead.

HIGHER LEVELS

Intermittently throughout the almost 200 year history of the Regatta, a crew comes along, makes an instantly extraordinary showing, and just as quickly fade from public memory. The Regatta is so rich in history that it is easy to forget that a teenage crew, the Higher Levels crew, once won the Regatta Championship.

Not only did they win top honours but won the Championship a second time and placed a respectable second place in a third Championship Race. The *Daily News* after the 1949 Regatta noted that this was the first time in Regatta history that an intermediate crew had won a Regatta Championship. The Higher Levels crew is also the only teenage crew ever to win a Regatta Championship.

The teen crew first rowed in the Regatta of 1949 in the Intermediate Race. The new Salter built boats from Oxford, England, had been placed on the Pond in 1948 and were not known for speed. In that year, although fair weather prevailed, not one crew rowed under the eleven minute mark. In 1949 the only crew to break that eleven minute barrier was the Higher Levels which recorded a time of 10:52.75 and 10:45.6 in the Championship.

Among those at Lakeside in 1949 to pay tribute to the teens was Dr. H. Rendell, who designed the *Blue Peter* and several other of the famous Sexton boats, and Jimmy Crotty who was marking his fiftieth year with the Regatta Committee. These two veterans observed that championship crews always came from the husky and strong muscled fishermen, truckers, and policemen.

The teens won the championships in 1949 and 1950, and came in second place in 1951 losing first place to the crew from the Waterford Hospital. Several of the crew had moved to the mainland in 1951 and had to arrange their holidays to get back to St. John's to participate in the Regatta. The 1951 crew included Jack Kenny, cox; L. Crane, stroke; B. Phelan; H. Crane; P. Moores; S. Kelloway; and A. LaFosse. (K. Connors had rowed the previous two years but not the 1951. He was replaced that year by A. LaFosse.)

HALL OF FAME

The Royal St. John's Regatta Committee has set up a Hall of Fame to honour the names of those who have made outstanding contributions to the Regatta since its beginning. The following is a list of those so far inducted into the Hall of Fame.

1987:
    Philip Brown, rower, coxswain
    James A. Clancy, builder
    Samuel Ebsary, rower/coxswain

Hon. Justice J. D. Higgins, builder
Hon. Justice W. J. Higgins, builder
John J. Kenny, coxswain
Lord Edward Morris, builder
Outer Cove crew 1901
Placentia Fishermen 1877
John J. Reardigan, rower, builder
Levi Rogers, coxswain
1901 Outer Cove Fishermen's crew

1988:

Gerald P. Angel and the Quidi Vidi Women's crew (1856)

1989:

Rendell W. Jeans, James A. Ring, and Robert Sexton

1990:

Hon. Sir Edgar Bowring, Gordon Tilley, John M. Tobin, and Arthur G. Williams, M.B.E.

1993:

James Carter, Jack Connors, Gerry Lewis, Ladies Hotel Newfoundland crew 1958: Albert Joy, cox; Bernice Lacey, stroke; Vera Smith; Jean Wilson; Patsy (Connolly) Leonard; Jean Dawe; Elsie Worthman; and Gerald 'Chick' Stone

1994:

John Coaker, Adrian O'Keefe, John O'Neill, and John Perlin.

1995:

The Blackhead crew 1904, Samuel Loveys, Alfred Holwell, Patrick Ring, and Geoffrey Stirling

<u>1996:</u>

Mike Dwyer, Tom Traverse, Gert Reardigan, the 1826 Committee, and the 1871 Committee

<u>1997:</u>

Cyril Boland, Alex Henley, the 1964 William Summers crew, and John Warren

<u>1998:</u>

Thomas Kearsey, Richard Squires, Thomas Stone, and the 1939 West End Police crew

<u>1999:</u>

Andrew Crosbie, Michael Howley, Mike Power, and the 1981 Smith-Stockley crew

<u>2000:</u>

Ed Hennessey, Max Dowden and the 1982 Outer Cove crew

<u>2001:</u>

John Barrington and the 1994 OZFM Female Championship crew

<u>2002:</u>

George Stockley, the Army Dock Male crew 1944-1948, and the Higher Levels Intermediate crew 1949-1950

REGATTA GREATS

One of most remarkable crews of Regatta history is the Butternut crew of 1997. In that year they achieved the kind of success that stands out in history and acts as an inspiration for generations to come. The powerful seven, after winning the Triple Crown of Newfoundland Regatta, amazed fans everywhere by setting a new Regatta record when they rowed the course in 8:57.14. (Triple Crown refers to winning the championships at the Placentia, Harbour Grace, and St. John's Regattas.) This marked the only time in Regatta history that a crew won the Triple Crown and set a new course record in the same year. The boat rowed by the Champions that memorable day was the *Good Luck*. Days before Regatta Day 1997, the Butternut crew recorded the time of 8:55 in practice.

Butternut crew making record time.

I had the honour of serving as Secretary of the Regatta Hall of Fame under the successive chairmanships of Bernard Collins and Don Wilson, which was followed by a term with the Board of Governors, chaired by Geoff Carnell with Don Johnson as Secretary.

The Butternut crew: L-R standing: Mel Rose, representing sponsor; Perry Cahill, stroke; Trevor Bonnell, representing sponsor; John Handrigan; and Shawn Budgell. L-R kneeling: Chris Barton; Gilbert Gibbons; Mike Jadine; and Mike Summers, cox.

While serving on the Committee I had the pleasure of researching and writing the nomination papers for ten candidates for the Hall of Fame. They were John Coaker, John O'Neill, the 1904 Blackhead crew, Samuel Loveys, Mickey Dwyer, Gert Reardigan, Cyril Boland, the William Summers Jr. crew, John Warren, and the 1939 West End Police.

Much more is to be written about the Regatta as history continues to be recorded at the event. The great names of rowers, coxswains, crews, and the builders of the last sixty years will be material for another volume on Regatta history. An important part of that history will be the participation of women in the Regatta which had been an exclusively male event from its start.

Author Jack Fitzgerald with Mrs. Cyril Boland holding the framed induction certificate of her husband at the Hall of Fame Dinner in 1997.

REPRINT OF THE *TELEGRAM*'S AUGUST 8, 1901,
COVERAGE OF THE ST. JOHN'S REGATTA
(REPRINTED WITH PERMISSION FROM THE *TELEGRAM*)

OUR ANNUAL DERBY DAY

HOW IT WAS CELEBRATED YESTERDAY—DELIGHTFUL WEATHER—CLOSELY CONTESTED RACES AND MUCH GENERAL ENJOYMENT

All the preparations which have been going on the past three months culminated yesterday in what we are pleased to call "our Derby" which is the first of all sports in Newfoundland. Everybody had been prepared for it and were looking forward to the good time they were going to have, and consequently an exodus of people commenced at 7 o'clock in the morning and continued up till late at evening, when much of the city was at the lakeside of Quidi Vidi. All business was suspended and the town itself looked as if it had been deserted pending a great catastrophe. At Quidi Vidi however, a great contrast was presented. The place was alive with spectators, all eager to see and hear about the races. Several tents had been temporarily erected on the grounds and considerable trade was done by the proprietors in the way of lunches, drinks, etc.

The weather was all that could be desired. Not a cloud was visible in the blue canopy of the heavens and the sun shone so hot that one could scarcely turn his eyes towards the skies for its dazzling brightness. Just a slight breeze was blowing which covered the lake with gentle ripples and added fourfold to its great natural beauty. A band, under the management of Prof. Power, was in attendance and occupied a stand erected expressly for them of bunting and decorated with the flags of the world's two greatest nations.

The crews of the various boats were in splendid form, which had been accomplished by their long and careful training. It was this very fact and that of the similarity of the boats which prevented even the best informed and the most interested to give any definite answer to the question ever and again being repeated-"Who is going to win the race?" As to the boats themselves: the one of course most talked of was the new *Blue Peter*, which was built a few weeks ago by the now famous "Bob" Sexton for Mr. W.C. Job. The boat which is conceded to be the best ever put on the lake, showed her superiority in the last race of yesterday, when she shot over the one and a half mile course to the stroke of the champions in 9:13 4/5. This is the quickest time in all the annals of our regattas that ever a boat has covered the course. Well, indeed, that Messrs. Job might feel proud of such a treasure, and "Bob's" little bit of modest pride is certainly excusable. It is said that he will find it difficult to beat his efforts in the construction of the *Blue Peter*, but as Bob improves every boat each successive year we will still wait for him to make his crowning effort.

The *Glance*, so popular last year was not in it this season. The *Red Cross*, though unlucky last year, comes up second in this Regatta. The *Bob Sexton, Daisy,* and remaining boats are considered to have "had their day." Shortly after 1 o'clock His Excellency the Governor arrived on the scene, while the band played the National Anthem. All our people feel proud of him and his friend Sir Charles Walpole, and will not forget the interest he has taken in all our sports. For the Committee themselves no praise can be too loud. Everything went off without a hitch. No difficulty was experienced in getting the boats to their positions, and no fouls or crosses of any sort were seen to mar the pleasure of the day. Betting and sweepstakes were largely indulged in, and the man with the "stakes" was very much in evidence and constantly enquired after. The races came of as follows:

Amateurs — At 10:40 a.m. the Amateurs lined up the buoys to the bugle call. The competing boats were the *Red Cross, Blue Peter, Bob Sexton, Glance* and *Daisy*. The Committee boat now rowed up the buoys and saw all boats in proper position. As the gun fired all made a dash and loud cheering arose from the spectators. At the start the *Bob Sexton* had the lead, but when only a few lengths from the buoy one of the rowlocks broke and she had to return to the boathouse. The *Daisy* and *Red Cross* were now ahead; before reaching the end of the pond however, the *Red Cross* had forced ahead and had an easy victory on the return. Her time was 9:40 4/5, which is the quickest Amateur time on record. In this race the *Glance* came in second and the *Daisy* and *Blue Peter* third and fourth, respectively.

Fishermen — This was a very hardly contested race. Near the lower end of the pond the *Glance*'s crew struck their oars against those of the *Blue Peter*, which some-what retarded the progress of both. The race was won by the *Red Cross* again in 9:30 4/5. The Blue Peter coming second.

Football — Three teams contested in this race. The Star, Fieldians and BIS in the *Blue Peter, Red Cross* and *Glance*, respectively. The Stars won, coming in, in 10:16 min-utes, and the Glance second in 10:19, there being not three feet difference in brows of the boats.

Labourers — This was a well rowed race. Four boats competed. The *Blue Peter* came in first. Her time was 9:43 with the *Bob Sexton* about three boat lengths behind, coming in in 10:53 4/5.

Brigades — This was the prettiest race of the day. Only two boats entered; the *Red Cross* (CCC), *Bob Sexton* (CLB). One can imagine how hardly contested it was when told that there was but a second and three-fifth difference between the arrival of the boats. The *Red Cross* won in 10:10 1/5.

An interval followed this race, during which his excellency presented the prizes as follows:

Amateurs — First, *Red Cross,* gold medals: J. Wallace, cox; H. Brownrigg; R. Simms; C.E. Jeffrey; L. Fowler; W. Ryan; and E. Murphy.

Fishermen — *Red Cross,* gold medals presented by the Governor: N. Gosse, cox; G. Tapper; J. Manning; F. Tapper; Jesse Manning; T. Clements; and J. Gosse.

Football — *Blue Peter,* gold medals: T. Wallace, cox; H. Brownrigg; W. Ryan; N. Vinnicombe; J. Brophy; E. Brophy; and E. Power.

Labourers — *Blue Peter,* $2 gold pieces presented by Hon. E.P .Morris: T. Whitten, cox; J. Flynn; S. Goody; F. Harvey; K. Whitten; J. Anthon; and J. Snow.

Brigade — *Red Cross,* silver cup presented by His Excellency the Governor: F.J. Donnelly, cox; J. Reddigan; J. Vinnicombe; J. Saterley; J. Mallard; R. Voisey; and J. Maher.

A short interval followed for the Committee to partake in a luncheon.

Mercantile — Four teams: Bowring's, Job's, Baine Johnston's, and Harvey's entered. There was more money out on this race than any other for the day. The *Blue Peter* (Job's) won in 9:38 1/5.

Juvenile — This race was not as interesting as the others. Five boats started, the *Glance* winning in 10:30 4/5.

Tradesmen — This was the second quickest race for the day, except the champions. The *Blue Peter* won in 9:31 2/5. The *Red Cross* coming second, *Sexton*, third and *Glance* fourth.

Truckmen — Three teams-East End, Central, and West End entered. The West End men won in the *Red Cross* in 10:04. The other boats were over three lengths behind.

Naval Reserves vs. Warships — The Naval Reserve boys in the *Red Cross* won this race against crews from the *Buzzard* and *Charybdis*. It was the hardest race of the day with the *Red Cross* being only about a foot ahead of the *Glance* which was rowed by a crew from the *Buzzard*. The *Red Cross* time was 10:20 1/5, the second boat being but fifth of a second behind her.

All-Comers — This race was only rowed from the bottom of the pond and was won by the *Red Cross* in 4:32. The *Bob Sexton* took second in 4:37.

Champions — The last and best race was for the championship of the pond. The *Blue Peter* won it in 9:13 4/5. The quickest time previous to this being 9:20 in the old *Myrtle*. The *Red Cross* was second in 9:22 3/5. The championship boat was rowed by the Outer Cove fishermen.